HEAL

– BEGIN WITH FOOD –

MELISSA DELPORT

HEAL

– BEGIN WITH FOOD –

MELISSA DELPORT

ACKNOWLEDGEMENTS

My mess has become my message and creating this book required me to truly dig deep. Deep into my emotional body, my physical energy and my creativity. This book has mirrored and created space for my healing and my hope is that it does this for you too.

HEAL would not have been possible without those who held me up throughout its creation:

Lauren, I am so deeply grateful to have you as my partner in life. To say that you are my rock, my guidance, my support and my inspiration is not enough. Thank you for every single moment of love and energy you give to me and my dreams. Words are not enough. You are the most remarkable human I know. I am forever changed and forever rearranged.

Mom, thank you for stepping up into not only your greatness and health, but also for shining your light my way. You are an incredible human being. To create this book with the woman who taught me all that I know in life and in the kitchen was a blessing and an honour. The memories made will be cherished for life. Always turn to the sun and know that deeper healing is yours.

Dad, thank you for your unwavering support and for teaching me to be fearless and relentless in building my dreams.

Nick and Hendre, I love you. Thank you for cheering me on, believing in me, and for showing me that anything is possible if you work hard enough and believe in yourself. Your zest for life is infectious.

To my team at Penguin Random House: Beverley, thank you for your calm energy and making any deadline seem possible. Joy, for working my voice into clarity, and Helen, for creating this book with me and turning it into something of which I am truly proud. It would not have been possible without you. Creating this vision is a dream come true.

To my friends and every single person who has supported me over the years, be it on social media, by buying a book or by offering simple words of encouragement, thank you for giving my dream a voice and allowing me to share my vulnerability with you. May you find the deeper healing on offer and know that you are worthy of great health.

Published in 2021 by Struik Lifestyle
(an imprint of Penguin Random House (Pty) Ltd)
Company Reg. No. 1953/000441/07
The Estuaries, 4 Oxbow Crescent, Century Avenue, Century City, 7441
P O Box 1144, Cape Town, 8000, South Africa

ISBN 978-1-43231-046-2

Publisher: Beverley Dodd
Managing editor: Cecilia Barfield
Editor and indexer: Joy Nel
Designer: Helen Henn
Photographer and food stylist: Melissa Delport
Food styling assistant: Sonja Delport
Proofreader: Bronwen Maynier
Make-up and hair (cover): Gina Maskell
Cover photographer: Luke Kuisis

Reproduction by Studio Repro and Hirt & Carter Cape (Pty) Ltd
Printed and bound in China by C&C Offset Printing Co., Ltd.

FSC
MIX
Paper from responsible sources
FSC™ C101537
www.fsc.org

CONTENTS

INTRODUCTION

This book is meant to be a book of celebration. A book that combines my love of food and healthy living. When I speak of health, I mean sleeping well, a happy digestive system, a calmer state of mind, balanced hormones and well-managed stress. In other words, the grey areas in life that aren't covered by a handbook.

When I started this journey with my first cookbook, *WHOLE – Bowl Food for Balance*, I realised that so many people were hungry. They were hungry for more information, more delicious food and, most importantly, to feel better within their bodies. We know fad diets don't work and we know (hopefully) that being thin is not the only goal. Health is the objective and living a healthy, balanced life comes down to two spheres within your life: primary food and secondary food. I first discovered these principles while studying to become a Holistic Health Coach and then furthered my understanding when I used these tools to find balance in my own life.

Let me explain a little more. Primary food is not food that you put into your mouth. This might sound strange because you would presume that what you put into your mouth is primary because it keeps you alive. However, it goes much deeper than this. Primary food is the soul food that feeds you – your career, spirituality, relationships, exercise, and areas within this space that nourish you.

If this concept is still not clear, let me put it to you this way. Take, for example, a high-powered, stressed-to-the-hilt career woman with an abusive spouse. She works 14-hour days, six days a week, and on the seventh gets no rest because her spouse is chewing her ear off about some perceived injustice. She can eat all the kale she wants and run 10 kilometres every morning, but her weight probably won't budge. Why? Because of multiple complex reasons from elevated cortisol in the system to stress-induced insomnia. On their own, calorie counting, food group deprivation and over exercising won't solve the problem (the partner or the weight).

So, what is the next step? How does she find balance? More importantly, how do you find balance?

My goal through this book is to help combine the primary with the additional sphere of secondary foods, the latter being the food you eat. I have done this by providing delicious recipes and asking thought-provoking questions that will have you look a little deeper into your primary foods and consider your life from a holistic approach.

To continue from the example above, when the career woman finally decides to solve things with her spouse and works towards finding a more restorative form of exercise (possibly Yin Yoga or active walks in the park) and perhaps sets healthy boundaries with her work, her body will feel safe, ultimately lowering her cortisol. Through these changes she will then find it easier to balance her food because her body won't be craving the most calorie-dense foods available.

Your body needs energy when you're stressed, so if you are trying to manage your food in a stressful state then you are looking at the puzzle incorrectly. Food isn't the problem, the stress is.

If you can relate at all to the woman in the example above, and you invite these changes into your life, you will become healthier. When you become healthier from a holistic approach you can find balanced weight. Make sense? Losing weight isn't just about the food, nor is it the primary goal.

I haven't even touched on the millions of dollars the food industry spends on the clever marketing of unhealthy food to you and your children and how that same industry is consciously making certain foods more addictive with chemicals that stimulate your brain the same way drugs would.

Their number one concern? Money, *not* your health.

Cheap, processed foods are sold on a massive scale to misinformed consumers and continue to provide a seemingly never-ending stream of revenue for these food giants. What's even worse is that these foods are being given to children, setting them up for a lifetime of bad habits and health problems.

I know this because I was one of those children. I was the overweight little girl who dealt with the difficult emotional, psychological and physical challenges that come with it.

I hear this so often: 'Healthy eating is expensive.' True AND false. TRUE, if you run to your local health store and buy every single superfood under the sun along with imported health products. FALSE, if you pop down to your local grocer or farmers' market to purchase a fresh, unprocessed butternut and go home and roast it in a little olive oil.

Ask yourself this: Do I want to spend the money now on eating healthily or later on while trying to fix my health? Lifestyle diseases, such as type 2 diabetes, high blood pressure and certain types of cancer, are not cheap.

The food you choose to eat can either support your health and your body's ability to heal, or it can do the opposite and damage it (sometimes irreversibly). It's so much bigger and deeper than just weight.

Food matters. And it obviously matters to you given that you have picked up this book. But it's not just any food, it's food that is real – mostly plant based, preservative free, organic as much as possible and cooked using healthier processes. And what matters just as much? Answer: This great thing called life and how we live it. How we balance all that is available to us from a holistic, healthy and loving approach.

You are so much more than a number on a scale or how thin you are. You are a multi-faceted, beautiful being and if you start to love your life and your body, everything can change. It's time to stand up to the bully in your head and leave the past behind you. You can heal and you can find balance with food and all other areas of your life. You are worthy of good health, in all aspects. The time has come for you to see that being healthy and being thin are not the same thing.

I have learnt through my own experience of connecting to my health and through my studies that our bodies naturally know what they need to do to heal. They are these beautiful machines that do exactly what they need to do to survive. If you accidentally cut yourself, you don't tell your body how to heal. Your body just heals. It's the same with intuitive, mindful eating.

My hope is for you to start to trust your body and to trust yourself in the kitchen. To eat real wholesome food. To not overthink it or ask for someone else's opinion, but rather to connect to a deeper knowing. A knowing that will guide you to good health and a journey that will connect you to yourself.

Now close your eyes and take a deep breath. Connect. Ask yourself, what do I feel like eating? And then turn the page and find the recipe to satisfy that need.

HEALTH AND WELLNESS

I am not a doctor. Any advice that I give in this book is through my own research and experience as a health coach. Please consult a healthcare practitioner before embarking on a new journey into replacing any medication or removing it completely.

Adaptogens are wonderful and have worked for me. My advice, when taking adaptogens or other supplements, is to start slowly and one at a time – under the care of a doctor, as I did – so you know what works for you. This consistency is key. If you are pregnant or breastfeeding, please consult your doctor *before* using these products.

A NOTE ON MEAT

Simply put, plants and trees have some of the most efficient systems on earth. Elegantly designed, harnessing the energy of the sun to photosynthesise, cycling ancient nutrients into life, and converting water and carbon dioxide into oxygen. We have the privilege of consuming these plants as optimal fuel for our bodies.

Eating cleaner results in increased energy, less brain fog and better sleep. For this reason, I have left the meat out of this book completely, focusing solely on plant-based recipes. However, I do advocate for listening to your body, so if eating meat aligns with you then do try to source sustainable meat, such as grass-fed and free-range, from your local butcher or farm. Listen to your body and if it tells you to add a meat companion to one of these recipes, then feel free to do so. Let your intuition guide you and use these recipes as a tool to experiment.

A NOTE ON DAIRY

I don't drink milk and seldom eat cheese as I have learnt that my body doesn't process it easily. What does your body like? Does dairy work for you? If so, try to keep it down to a maximum of three times a week and focus on organic, ethical white cheeses when you do decide to have some. Ricotta, feta and goat's milk cheese are usually the go-to options in my kitchen. If you are vegan, leave out the dairy completely and experiment with nutritional yeast, which tastes just like cheese. And whether you are vegan or not, I suggest trying oat milk, nut milks and even coconut milk as a substitute to your daily milk intake.

EXPLORING AYURVEDA

This is not an Ayurvedic cookbook. I have, however, drawn inspiration from and used some basic principles of Ayurvedic practices which allowed me to listen to my body seasonally and even daily, and supported me to good health.

Ayurveda is a holistic health system that is over 3 000 years old, with its roots in India. It is born of the belief that health and wellness are based on a delicate balance between mind, body and spirit.

The following explanation of Ayurveda is by no means exhaustive. If you find some of the information resonates with you, I encourage you to delve further into existing studies and books on this ancient practice to seek a deeper understanding.

Followers of Ayurveda believe that every person is made up of five basic elements found in the universe: space, air, fire, water and earth. These combine in the body to form three life forces or energies, called doshas. Doshas control how your body works. There is Vata dosha (space and air), Pitta dosha (fire and water) and Kapha dosha (water and earth).

Everyone inherits a unique mix of the three doshas, but one is usually more prominent than the others. It is believed that your chances of getting sick and the health issues you develop are linked to the balance of your doshas. If you're interested in finding out more, there are a number of online sources that can help you identify your doshas. Once you understand and discover what dosha you are, you can learn how to eat and move to keep yourself in balance throughout the seasons.

Ayurveda also has an eloquent explanation for inflammation (fire) and the journey to disease. Simply put, disease is really a chronic state of inflammation. In other words, if inflammation is left untreated for long enough, it becomes chronic. Therefore, it is more important to focus on catching the problem early to prevent its inevitable progression towards disease rather than treating its symptomatic manifestation with long-term medication.

Eating inflammatory and processed foods high in sugar or sodium feeds inflammation. And if you eat these foods for long enough and in sufficient quantities while neglecting your health, what do you get? Chronic inflammation, which can manifest as arthritis, skin rashes, ulcers, diabetes, high blood pressure, IBS (irritable bowel syndrome), and a plethora of other illnesses and diseases.

The good news is that you can reverse a multitude of ailments within weeks of eating more healthily, and ultimately feel better for it while you heal.

Looking after our gut and digestive health is critical for overall health. In Ayurveda, agni is your digestive fire, or your digestion strength, and is the basis of good health. When I ask you to tune into your body, I want you to try to tune into your digestion.

Did you find that you were bloated after a certain meal? Did you get heartburn or feel tired? Try to listen to your body and see how you feel after eating a certain meal or food type. If you are feeling sluggish, include fresh greens with your next meal or eat something lighter. If you have stomach cramps, a warm, cooked meal, such as a soothing, hearty lentil soup or a kitchari (see page 127), could work better for your body. Not only are these meals delicious, but they are also gentle on the digestion and provide healing benefits with the selection of spices used.

In Ayurveda, there are six tastes known as Shad Rasa, and I try to incorporate all six of these tastes into every dish I create. What are they?

SWEET – usually the bulk of the meal in the vegetables and grains.

SOUR – citrus, such as lime or lemon.

SALTY – Himalayan salt.

PUNGENT – black pepper, mustard, chilli.

ASTRINGENT – turmeric.

BITTER – kale, spinach, parsley or coriander.

I want to focus on the bitter taste specifically since it is the one that is most often left out of meals or diets altogether. The bitter taste has a *lekhana* function, meaning it acts by scraping fat and toxins from the body. It is also anti-parasitic, reduces burning sensations or skin eruptions, and helps to cleanse the liver. So, if there is one thing I would love for you to achieve with this cookbook, it is that you eat more Tikta (read: fresh greens) regardless of your dosha. Dark leafy greens are incredibly good for you.

If you alter your diet and clean up your eating, it is possible to not need medication and still live symptom free from many ailments.

Food is medicine and it's time we start to see it as such. It has the ability to heal. It has the ability to fight inflammation and support the immune system. Healthy fats can support the central nervous system, and a plant-based diet can aid cancer-fighting cells and combat type 2 diabetes. It is possible to change your lifestyle, eat healthier, move your body more, feel the sunshine on your skin, laugh, and even lessen the need for many of the medications we are so easily prescribed today. Nature is its own pharmacy – are you willing to tap in?

DIGESTION
You are what you eat. Even more so, you are what you absorb.

There is a huge difference between assimilation of nutrients and digesting your food. So, if you haven't heard it before: Chew, chew, chew your food! Many of us rush through our meals without leaving a second for the mind-body connection to happen. When you chew your food, you start the process of digestion. You are breaking down the food and your saliva assists in this process. Chewing your food ensures that you are not only going to be digesting it properly but it also prevents you from overeating. You will be doing your body a huge favour by allowing yourself more time to enjoy your meals. You will be amazed at how much smaller the portion sizes are that your body actually needs and desires. Savour the texture and flavour of your meal as much and as often as possible. Looking after your gut is essential to good health.

Did you know that a major portion of our nervous system is located in our intestines? Western doctors call it the Enteric Nervous System (ENS), but it's also commonly known as the 'second brain'. The ENS is the reason for that 'gut feeling' we sometimes get, because the ENS can operate independently of the brain, spinal cord and central nervous system. For example, scientists were astounded to learn that about 90 per cent of the fibres in the primary nerve, known as the vagus nerve, carry information from the gut to the brain and not the other way around. Those moments when we feel butterflies in our stomach, or suddenly get an intuitive hit on what to do in a moment of danger, or a powerful feeling about someone, all stem from our 'second brain'.

Another significant fact is that 90 per cent of the body's serotonin is produced in the gut, as well as about 50 per cent of the body's dopamine. These chemicals are responsible for sleep, memory, metabolism and emotional wellbeing. Additionally, your intestines produce and co-regulate 30 other neurotransmitters identical to those found in your brain which are used by the central nervous system to regulate our hormones, mood, stress levels, sleep patterns, mental functioning and a number of other essential body processes. These all point to the realisation that the gut is incredibly important for a number of functions that we're only recently starting to understand.

If you want to ensure that you have a gut-friendly diet, then focus on natural high-fibre raw foods and greens, along with plenty of water and healthy fats. Unfriendly bacteria and a surplus of yeast in the gut can be caused by excess meat, dairy, refined sugar or processed foods. This is how we end up with indigestion, irritable bowel syndrome and bloating.

I encourage you to try to eat as much *live* food as possible and as often as you can. By live food, I mean raw or naturally fermented foods. To further support your digestive function you can also try milk thistle, dandelion and artichoke leaf, taken as a supplement and found at your local health store. I also include a daily probiotic into my diet and take it first thing in the morning on an empty stomach. Make sure you buy one that needs to be stored in the fridge and try to buy the best quality recommended by your local health shop. Probiotics are wonderful at alleviating the symptoms of irritable bowel syndrome, bloating and toxin build-up in the system.

We also cannot neglect how our emotional and mental states impact our gut health. When we are anxious, we feel it in our stomach or perhaps lose our appetite. When we are stressed, it can cause us to eat quicker, which can cause stomach pain. This is why mindful eating and being aware of our emotional state can have a positive impact. At the start of each chapter I ask a few questions to encourage you to check in and catch your breath before cooking and eating. Take the time to consider the questions and delve into the pattern of your answers.

A NOTE ON HIGH-FIBRE FOODS

When you move onto healthier foods that are high in fibre (such as beans, lentils and chickpeas) your digestive system and gut bacteria, which is often used to soft processed foods, needs time to become accustomed to digesting the long-chain carbohydrates. This means that it will take a little while for your gut microbiome to establish. The more you feed the healthy bacteria, the stronger they become. So, if you experience bloat or gas when initially eating lentils, this is perfectly normal if you don't usually eat these foods. I encourage you to eat them more regularly over the period of two weeks and to check in with your body. If discomfort continues, then food sensitivities may be coming into play. Eating fibre-rich foods builds a stronger digestive system that not only can digest beans and other new high-fibre real foods, but also heals the damage caused by processed sugary foods.

I suggest soaking dried lentils, beans and chickpeas overnight before cooking them. This halves the cooking time as well as assists the digestive system. Take time to cultivate your inner garden and turn it into a rainforest of healthy bacteria.

BLOOD SUGAR AND ENERGY

We all know what it is like to be on a caffeine or sugar high and have all the energy in the world. We also know that as soon as that supply runs out we are left feeling worse for wear. Symptoms such as fatigue and headaches can kick in, which leave us wanting more sugar or caffeine. Essentially you will be in a washing machine on the repeat cycle.

The good news is that there is this wonderful world out there where you are able to have an abundant supply of natural energy that doesn't pick you up and smash you down. Balancing your blood sugar also means fewer mood swings, which results in not only a happier day for you but a happier day for those around you as well as healthier eating habits. You can change the repeat cycle to a sustainable and positive one.

There are many health problems today that can be traced to sugar imbalances due to unhealthy food choices. The refined sugars and processed foods such as biscuits, chocolates, cakes, fizzy and sugary drinks, white pasta, bread and rice, and hidden sugars in health foods are digested very quickly and will leave you with unwanted highs and headaches, an insulin surge and then, of course, the crash, more accurately known as hypoglycemia. That's when you get the 3pm slump that results in you wanting to reach for the coffee and slab of chocolate in your desk drawer.

Do you see the pattern? This dangerous cycle can lead to heart disease and the dreaded type 2 diabetes arising in your life.

Instead, set yourself up with a steady supply of energy through complex carbohydrates, beans, pulses, whole grains, fruits and vegetables. This will allow you to have more natural and sustainable mental and physical energy.

Also, removing sugar, alcohol and caffeine from your diet will result in you feeling better and lessening your chances of costly health problems later on. The wonderful news? It doesn't have to be forever. It is just to kick start you on this journey of health. Try it out for two weeks and see how you feel. Then, after that, I recommend one morning coffee and the odd glass of wine. This is balance and it is achievable.

I don't want you to have a diet mentality of removing entire food groups from your diet forever and then three days later binging on the exact food group you tried to remove. If you are a fad-dieter then you know what I am talking about. You also know that it never works in the long run. You are not defined by a number on a scale. Let's focus on health. Balanced weight will come. It's an amazing and welcome side effect of being healthy and looking after yourself!

FOOD SENSITIVITY

I want to share a story with you. When I was a fad-dieter, I used to fear carbs and restrict myself all the time. It resulted in me having severe anxiety around food and more often than not skipping meals as I believed if I ate less then I would get thin. The result? I would wake up in the middle of the night starving and make my way to the fridge on autopilot. I was so hungry that I ate anything that was in my line of sight. When I was dieting, I was eating meat such as a cured ham because I believed high protein was good for me. I started to have anxiety around this behaviour and then decided that if I left a bag of carrots in the fridge it would be my safety net for eating something healthy. Night after night I would devour midnight carrots in front of the fridge due to my hunger pangs from starving myself.

Fast forward to a few years later when I started my health journey and discovered that I suffered from leaky gut and had sensitivity to raw food due to a weak digestive system. Eating one carrot would cause so much bloat and pain that I actually stopped eating raw carrots until I had healed.

The point of my story is that if you have never felt different then you won't know what food sensitivities or intolerances you may have. The only way of finding out is to wipe the slate clean with healthy basics, lay the foundation of good health, have a curious open mind and to learn from and listen to your body.

Food sensitivities and intolerances are a very common problem today and many people have probably lived with them for years without knowing what is causing their ailments. The most common culprits are dairy, wheat (gluten), soy, shellfish, peanuts and yeast. Improving your digestive function, enhancing your immune system and supporting your general health through whole food eating can reduce your food sensitivities. I also suggest rotating your food and not eating too much of one thing while combining this with 'eating through the rainbow'. Pick a variety of fruits and vegetables and focus on different colours and cooking styles. This will not only make healthy food fun and beautiful and expand your cooking skill set, but will also allow your taste buds to journey through the wonderful and diverse flavours on offer.

Healthy eating takes practice. If you have a palate that grew up with packaged foods, bottled sauces and refined carbs, of course it will taste different at first. Give it a chance and before you know it those refined and processed foods that were once so familiar will truly taste like the unhealthy pseudo-foods that they are. If you think you may suffer from any food intolerances then I urge you to explore this more fully, eliminating them individually to see which ones impact your body. Intolerances can show up through inflammation, which presents in heartburn, skin rashes, irregular bowel movements and weakened immunity.

HEART AND BLOOD CIRCULATION

There is always something to be grateful for on this journey into health and healing. I know my beating heart is something I celebrate daily. Why? It never skips a beat and is delivering vital blood and nutrients to my body through a miraculous highway that is my cardiovascular system. My body receives oxygen and removes carbon dioxide and waste and does it all without me even thinking about it.

Yours does the same and that is why it is so important to look after it. Hiding behind genetics isn't going to cut it. Just because your father suffered from heart disease doesn't mean you will automatically suffer the same degenerative fate, it only means you need to pay more attention to what your individual risk factors are and make choices that support you in minimising that risk.

So, how is it possible to do that with diet? The reality is, changing your eating habits will make a significant difference in lowering risk, and how you choose to nourish your body should be a priority. For example, turning your attention to foods low in saturated fats, sugar and refined carbohydrates and including foods high in complex carbohydrates, such as grains, fresh vegetables and fruits, is a great start. Drink plenty of water and supplement your daily water intake by including herbal teas for a change of pace (and temperature).

Minimise your consumption of alcohol and caffeinated teas and coffee that are too often accompanied by generous helpings of dairy milk and sugar. High blood pressure and cholesterol are common issues in our modern lifestyle, which are only exacerbated by our predilection for quick fixes and instant results. This is where the doctor's prescription fits into the equation. The insanity of it all is that we are taking pills for the symptom and not addressing the root cause. Our food.

Pills alone will not save us or fix the problem and it's time we realise this. If you look after your body and health, it is possible to reduce if not eradicate altogether the exorbitant amount you could be spending on medication every month and feeling as if you've received a life sentence. You don't have to live a life on a variety of medications. But this is only a possibility if you choose to change your lifestyle.

HORMONES

Hormones, the magical little workers that send your cells messages that no one can actually see, yet play such a vital part in our wellbeing, are truly the unsung heroes of a healthy, functioning system.

Although most of the clients I work with in finding hormonal health are women, hormonal health is also applicable to men. Looking after our hormones means we look after how we age, feel, deal with stress and even our sexual performance.

You don't have to be at the mercy of hormonal imbalances that result in fatigue, limited sexual drive or hormonal acne. Hormonal health is achievable without oral contraceptives and, to be honest, you will feel so much better. Don't get me wrong, oral contraception has its place and it is your choice whether to use it or not. There is zero judgement here, but the reality is it is often prescribed as a solution to a much deeper problem. It is like putting a plaster over a deep wound. Looking after your hormones means healthier fertility, beautiful clear skin, increased energy, and a solution to many inflammatory problems such as polycystic ovarian syndrome (PCOS).

I was diagnosed with PCOS when I was 17 and thought it was a life sentence. PCOS affects one in eight women of child-bearing age and the prognosis isn't a good one: acne, weight gain, infertility and a high risk of ovarian cancer and diabetes. I thought my life was over. Well I am here to tell you that it is not a sentence and with diet and lifestyle, changes in hormonal health are achievable. Using food as medicine, my symptoms have been in remission and I now have a regular monthly cycle. Focusing on a diet that offers enough essential fatty acids, eating fibre-rich foods, staying hydrated, and removing things such as oestrogenic-high dairy, meats, soft plastics and pesticides will support your hormonal health. Equally important is staying away from fried, processed and saturated fatty foods such as margarine, meats and processed dairy.

THYROID AND METABOLISM

The thyroid is a powerful organ that controls how quickly your body burns energy. Furthermore, your whole body will slow down if you do not have enough thyroid hormone. This includes your blood pressure, circulation, energy levels, metabolism and temperature. If you make too much of the thyroid hormone, your body will go into hyperdrive. Looking after the thyroid is critical to good health and nourishing it through foods is possible. Foods that are good for the thyroid are foods that are high in iodine, such as seaweed, and the amino acid tyrosine. Choose foods that are high in selenium, calcium, zinc and vitamins A, C, E and B-complex. Complete proteins and essential fatty acids are also critical to thyroid health and can be found in chia seeds, walnuts and kidney beans to name a few. I explore all these foods in the recipes to come and I encourage you to do the same.

MOVE YOUR BODY: BALANCE YOUR MIND AND EMOTIONS

Looking after our emotional and mental health plays a critical role in achieving physical health.

To reduce the intricacies and contributors of physical health to a 'don't eat carbs' mentality doesn't make sense and, aside from being a gross oversimplification, is tied to the toxic diet mentality of getting thin. That black-and-white way of thinking needs an overhaul. We all have our pasts and they aren't always pretty. That's okay. There is nothing wrong with seeking support in the form of therapy and unpacking past traumatic experiences. You are not weak for it.

I don't think we talk about mental and emotional well-being often or seriously enough. Trauma is relative and each person's journey is personal. In order to move past the past we need to move through it, and this can only be done by unpacking it. It can be scary. It can hurt and even make us feel unsafe. But the truth of the matter is that these fears and anxieties often result in overeating as a coping mechanism to overwhelming emotions or in our digestive system shutting down or tripping us up around each corner.

What is lying deeper, underneath your emotional self and your eating habits? Perhaps it's a parent who picked on you because of your weight. Perhaps it's wanting to be skinny like the people on mainstream and social media. Whatever it is, you are not a failure for it and so many people are in the same boat. We just don't talk about it enough. Learning to sit with difficult emotions and becoming a strong container for all that you have been through takes time.

Moving your body with gentle exercise regularly is critical not only to physical wellbeing but to your emotional and mental wellbeing as well. It supports stress relief and releases endorphins, which promote happiness. Looking after your brain and your gut from a nutritional aspect makes a huge difference too. Dopamine, adrenaline and serotonin are largely the result of the food and air we consume. If you are eating a poor diet and not moving your body, then you are creating an environment for depression, anxiety and chemical imbalances.

So many children these days are glued to cellphones, eating brown food with no nutritional value that comes from a box and, to be honest, the grown-ups aren't far behind. Eating nutritionally dense food, connecting emotionally to your inner landscape and feeling the sunshine on your skin is part of the bigger picture of health and wellbeing. I hope to encourage you to look deeper. What is really going on for you? How are you teaching your children to look after themselves and interact with their emotions?

"I believe that depression is legitimate but I also believe that if you don't exercise, eat nutritious food, get sunlight, get enough sleep, consume positive material, surround yourself with support then you aren't giving yourself a fighting chance." - Anon.

DETOXIFICATION

Don't panic. Many people read the word 'detox' and think they won't be able to have a joyful life because they will be living on green juice and carrot sticks. This is NOT the case. Living a life with less toxins can be done while your food is in abundance.

There are many ways that we can detox our bodies. The skin, liver, lungs, kidneys and bowels are the way we rid our bodies of pesticides, chemicals, food additives, herbicides and preservatives, and looking after these systems is critical to good health.

There are so many toxins in our environment, from the air we breathe and the food we eat and drink to the surfaces we touch and the substances and products we use. The reality is that when you have absorbed too many toxins, they will start to damage your organs. Taking stock of our exposure to our environment is the only way we are able to understand its impact and is the first step in getting it under control.

How often and well our bowels operate is also critical to good overall health and hormonal balance. You should have an easy evacuation at least once a day without the use of coffee or laxatives. If this isn't the case then the balance is off somewhere, and the reality is that you will immediately feel it in your energy levels and your general wellbeing. Eating a diet that is high in fibre with ample hydration is important. Focus on brown rice, dark leafy greens, fruits and beans to name a few.

If you are eating processed foods that are high in sugars and refined carbohydrates you will feed the bad bacteria in your gut. This bacteria is responsible for irregular bowel movements. Meat and eggs have zero fibre so although they can be part of a balanced diet, they do not aid gut health.

To support the good bacteria in your gut you need to include live foods such as kimchi, sauerkraut and miso, as well as vitamin B in your diet. You do not want to heat or cook these foods as the good bacteria will die. Try to get a product that is organic and read the label to ensure that it doesn't have hidden chemicals or sugars.

To look after your skin, you can use chemical-free creams and rather opt for a body oil that has essential oils in it. I also include dry brushing into my weekly routine, which removes old skin cells and stimulates the lymphatic system, aiding in fighting cellulite (you don't need to be ashamed of this, we all have it). It's also immensely therapeutic and an act of self-love. Drinking plenty of water supports our kidneys and staying away from cigarette smoke looks after our lungs.

STRESS

Stress is one of the hardest things to manage. We all have it and we cannot stop life from happening. However, we can learn the rules of engagement with stress and learn to manage it better by using practical tools such as gentle exercise.

As humans, we are incredibly adaptive. The problem lies in the levels of cortisol in our bodies due to stress – stress leads to high levels of cortisol, and high levels of cortisol lead to weight gain or prevent weight loss – so if you want to find balanced weight you need to find a way to manage stress better. One of the biggest supports for stress management is to focus on drinking less caffeinated coffee. Caffeine fires up our adrenal glands and although it is not to be demonised, excessive coffee or coffee on an empty stomach can wreak havoc on an already stressed system. Making better food choices and lifestyle changes will help you manage stress better. Good nutrition will also support your energy levels.

I have clients who have a handle on situations that would have previously caused them untold stress because now they have the energy to manage a life of abundance.

Cutting down on coffee, flipping the switch and consuming nutritious food are helpful ways of managing stress. But what else can you do? A stressed body needs vitamins C and B, zinc, potassium and magnesium. These vitamins are always best in their natural state as the body knows how to process natural food. That being said, additional support through supplementation can be a good thing too. Make sure to find a brand of supplements that is not filled with colourants and is sugar and starch free.

Going for regular, low-intensity exercise – preferably in nature – is critical. A 30-minute walk four times a week will be glorious for not only your physical stress but your mental health too. Prioritise yourself and make the time. It's part of self-care. The only way you will ever be able to take control of your stress and health is to start to care about yourself and carve out the 'me' time that a balanced lifestyle demands.

Yoga and deep breathing exercises are also beneficial. Breathe in through your nose, deep into your belly, for four counts and then release this breath slowly through your nose again for another four counts. This should be repeated three times, at least once a day. Deep breathing allows our body and mind to reset, even if just for a minute.

Prioritising sleep is non-negotiable. Sleep is the most important time for your body to rest and restore. The hours between 9pm and 12am are also the most important. Slow down on social media, especially before bedtime – staying up till midnight looking at a bright screen on your phone affects your circadian rhythm. Perhaps you should ask yourself this: is it adding any significant value to my life? Rather do deep belly breathing, drink herbal tea such as chamomile, and read a book before bed to allow the mind and body to wind down more naturally and get ready for sleep.

The vagus nerve is the tenth cranial nerve and one of its many functions is our parasympathetic nervous system function. It controls our digestion, respiration and heart rate functioning. Connecting to our breath and deep breathing calms the vagus nerve, in turn telling our body it is safe. This is crucial for good sleep, digestion and life. So breathe!

IMMUNITY

Your body is a glorious working machine that is fighting free radicals, bacteria and viruses every day. Your immune system is behind this battle and the best way to look after your soldiers is through proper nutrition and focusing on a variety of nutrient-dense foods. Arming your immune system with vitamins C, A and E and antioxidants that fight free radicals is a way to support your immune system. In other words, eating citrus and a variety of nuts and seeds along with legumes and (my personal favourite) good-quality dark chocolate, which contains iron, magnesium and zinc, is fundamental to supporting a strong immune system.

Including vitamin B and selenium in your arsenal along with omega-3 and -6 essential fatty acids can help to support the control of inflammation, while garlic and onions can increase your intake of allicin, an antibacterial, antiviral and antifungal substance. Sprouted broccoli and shiitake mushrooms are wonderful as added immune support. I hope you start to get the picture. Eating a variety of whole real foods builds you up to good health from the inside out. Give all these different foods a go.

BE A CONSCIOUS CONSUMER

It goes without saying that the world is in desperate need of people who are willing to vote with their wallet and who believe every little change helps. Between the climate crisis, global pandemics, dwindling natural resources and the devastating pollution in our oceans, we are facing a serious catastrophic event – our extinction.

I believe each and every one of us has the power and the responsibility to save the planet and we can do so through our kitchens. Recycle your food plastics if you have them (they are sometimes unavoidable), and compost your food waste to use in your garden. Shop organic, local and seasonal produce as much and as often as possible, and take a reusable shopping bag with you when you do. Fill your glass jars at your local grocer to avoid packets and

support the little grocers promoting plastic-free shopping. When you are weighing your food at the fresh produce section, does it really need a plastic bag that will go in a plastic bag later or can they just weigh it as is? So many gorgeous fruits and vegetables are already in their own glorious packaging designed over millions of years by Mother Nature herself. How could we possibly improve on the banana peel? Or mango skin? We already need to wash our fruit and vegetables, so the additional packaging is really not needed.

If we vote with our wallets then we are going to bring down the price of eco-friendly and earth-conscious products and we can start to get cautiously optimistic that the corporations that wish to survive the consumerist revolution will see the value in healthy real food and less-harmful packaging and plastic.

I'm sure you have heard it a million times before, but never before has it carried the weight it does in a post-Covid-19 world: We have to be the change we want to see in the world, no matter how big or small. I don't always get it right and you don't have to either, but pretending there isn't a problem and doing nothing is no longer an option.

I can save the world through this cookbook in my own small way. So can you. Sometimes it's about propagating an idea which then becomes a movement. When we know better, we have to do better and I believe that if you are reading this, you have a sense that the status quo needs an overhaul. Things need to change. Be an activist for change and teach people to do the same.

GET BEHIND YOUR CRAVINGS

What is your body telling you? Your cravings are real and are your body's way of trying to communicate with you. When we give in to these cravings, it's generally to go for something quick and that usually isn't nutritious.

Have you ever heard the saying, 'What you resist persists'? The more you dismiss and fight the craving, the louder the voice in your head is going to become. So, rather than trying to switch it off, why not try to understand it? It's not about powering through the craving or expecting yourself to have superhuman willpower to overcome it.

Sugar lights up the same part of the brain that cocaine does. This bodily response leaves you powerless to the cravings because of its addictive nature. Also, cravings can often be triggered by negative emotions or experiences. In these instances, changing your perspective can make the world of difference. Rather than thinking 'I am tired; I really need chocolate right now', try 'I am having the thought that I am tired and I really need chocolate right now'. Then, go

one step further and try 'I am noticing that I am having the thought that I am tired and I really need chocolate right now'. Do you see what this does? It creates space between your thoughts, and it's this distance that gives us the power to choose.

You can either act on the craving, satisfy the craving with something healthier, or let the craving pass. The simple fact is that we don't all act on every thought we have.

The other part of the craving is that your body might be missing vital nutrients. Certain cravings mean certain things and if you are working towards living a life of balance then go in with a curious mind and see, where are you at in your life? What have you been eating less of and what could you be in need of?

Here are some basic cravings, what they could mean, and a solution to try:

Craving	Possible shortage	Food fix
Chocolate	Magnesium	Dark leafy greens or dark chocolate
Meat and eggs	Iron	Beetroot, spinach, lean protein
Fatty foods	Essential fatty acids	Avocado, almonds, coconut oil
Savoury carbohydrates	Low energy	Root vegetables such as sweet potatoes, or apples and bananas
Sugar	Quick energy or dehydration	Greek yoghurt with berries, dark chocolate, water
Salty foods	Lack of electrolytes due to stress	Nuts, seeds, whole grains, fruits and vegetables

COOKING WITH INTUITION

I often get asked how I created a dish. To be honest, the dish created itself. I was just tasting and trusting as I went along and giving the dish the love it deserved. I don't want to eat a quick convenient meal that sacrifices on flavour, texture and health. Sacrifice these things often enough and you will end up riddled with inflammation.

Now I know we don't all have three hours a day to cook, but you can find the time twice a week to cook a decent meal and, when you do, cook a little extra. Voila! Meal prep.

Freeze the extra for the days you aren't able to cook. Soups and broths freeze well and if you heat them and add a little live food such as spinach, sprouts and kimchi you have a hearty, healthy meal in less than 10 minutes.

Fall in love with cooking and fall in love with food. It is what fuels you and what keeps you healthy. Save the convenience for 20 per cent of your life when you are at a party and you're eating pizza and sipping champagne.

Taking the time to cook is the only way to take control of your health. Be inspired by food and view it as energy. Good healthy food is positive energy that can help you get through ailments, protect you from colds, help you work through IBS and sail through menopause. All you need to do is open up in mind, body and spirit.

MEAL PREP

There are two approaches to this. Option 1 is doing meal prep on a Saturday or Sunday and then planning dinners around a bit of a schedule for the week ahead. This option is probably more suited to those with limited time.

Option 2 is cooking a little bit extra every dinner to provide for lunch the next day and may suit someone who enjoys cooking more often. Although freezing food is a helpful technique when it comes to meal prep and preventing food waste, I don't believe that eating frozen food too often is good for you. Fresh food has fresh energy and packs a punch.

My advice? Find what works for you. Tune into your body, and pay attention to how you feel with certain types of meal prep and what works best.

When it comes to meal prep, setting yourself up for success is key. From the correct cooking utensils right down to the storage containers in your fridge and freezer. I try to store my food in glass containers, which makes the contents easy to identify for quick assembly and access.

When I defrost a meal, I include a handful of dark leafy greens, such as kale that I've just cooked or fresh baby spinach, and add it while I'm warming the meal. On average, food can keep for up to a month in the freezer.

In the *For the little ones* chapter you will see some wholesome and easy meals for children and toddlers. It often requires so much effort to make meals for the adults and separate ones for the kids, but it's possible to do both with minimal effort. When you're prepping your own meals, prep for the kids at the same time. For example, when you're chopping up veggies for a soup, check the recipes for baby food and prep them as well. Where you can, try to switch in some real, fresh ingredients rather than bottled baby food, which can often have hidden sugars and preservatives.

KITCHEN AND HOME SPACE

Let's talk about setting your kitchen up for success. No one wants to cook in a space they dread walking into. Remember that making your space the best possible version of itself can take time and that's okay. As and when you can, build a collection of beautiful items that are sustainable and are a solid investment into your cooking space.

Here are a few things to consider changing in your space:

A snack cupboard filled with chips and chocolates is not only unhealthy for you, but unhealthy for your family too. It sets you up for failure. Repack this cupboard with healthy treats and snacks that you can indulge in mindfully and which are nutritious for your body. You will feel better for it.

The same goes for the fridge door that is filled to the brim with bottled sauces that are more than likely already expired. Clean out the fridge and organise it. Read labels and remove the products that are filled with chemicals and sugars.

Once you have finished with the fridge, move on to the pantry. I store all my nuts, seeds and grains in glass jars and arrange them so that I feel proud when I open my cupboards. This supports overall wellbeing in the kitchen space and makes healthy cooking fun.

You will also find that if you do a kitchen clean out and take control of your space, when you pick a recipe to cook you will know where everything is and can quickly identify if there are any missing ingredients that warrant a quick trip to the store.

Apply the environment that you want from your kitchen to the rest of your home. When we create a happy environment, it supports all aspects of health. A simple act like making your bed, packing away your clothes, washing up and opening the curtains can truly lift spirits and are little acts of kindness towards yourself that are needed daily.

Explore environmentally-friendly products and those that use fewer chemicals. Not only does your skin come into contact with these chemicals, but you breathe them in too. Read the labels on everything and make sure they are not harmful to us, our animals or our planet.

Try to surround yourself with inspiring people who bring positivity into your life. Nurturing relationships and making sure that we are supported by those around us is part of health. No one is an island. This works the other way around too. Support those less fortunate than you. Shop at your local, small-scale businesses and connect with those that you love. A simple phone call can go a long way.

KITCHEN EQUIPMENT
Here are my top recommendations when it comes to equipment in your kitchen space. They help make my job easier and make a real difference in the kitchen environment and when preparing meals.

BLENDER
When I use a blender in this book it is more often than not a NutriBullet or a high-speed food processor. They are wonderful tools that support healthy cooking and are a solid investment. When purchasing a new one, try to get the strongest wattage you can afford as these machines work hard and can often cut cooking time in half.

STOVE AND OVEN
This appliance is essential in your kitchen space as it supplies the heat that you need for cooking and baking. I prefer cooking on gas as it gives me better control. If you are a serious cook, then I suggest investing in a gas top/electric oven combination. Take note that the back of the oven is hotter than the front due to the door opening. Position your baking trays and roasting tins on the middle shelf, and be sure to turn them halfway through the roasting time. When baking, use the middle position in the middle of the shelf.

KNIVES
Buy a set of sharp knives that make food preparation easy and quick. At home I use a chef's knife, paring knife, vegetable knife, serrated knife and bread knife. This combination should cover all bases.

POTS
You will need at least one large one and a slightly smaller one. I have a variety of cast-iron and heavy-based steel pots. They are useful for dinner parties, meal prep or soups and sauces.

FRYING PANS

I suggest investing in a few different sizes. Try to get ones with oven-safe handles so that you can pop them into the oven when the recipe calls for it. I suggest using cast-iron or stainless-steel pans where possible.

GRATER AND PEELER

A sharp grater and peeler gets the job done and will save time in the kitchen.

TONGS

I use tongs often as they're a great tool for grilling and giving extra control when you're cooking over a high heat. They're not just for braaiing, so give them a try in the kitchen if you have a spare set lying around.

COLANDER

A colander is a necessity when it comes to washing vegetables and greens; it's not just for draining pastas.

CHOPPING BOARD

Try to get your hands on a thick wooden chopping board as this won't dull or blunt your knives like granite or ceramic will do. They can be rather expensive (add it to your birthday or Christmas wishlist), but are a good investment as they can last a lifetime if you care for them correctly. Avoid soaking or drenching wooden products as they can swell and warp. Whenever possible, wipe down with a damp cloth and cleaning agent wjth natural sanitising properties, such as salt and lemon, leave to dry and then rub with a little olive oil. You can also invest in plastic boards for fish and meat. Although less glamorous, they do last well.

FOR THE PANTRY

SUPERFOODS

You will find a variety of superfoods in this book. What are they? Superfoods are powerful, nutritious and mineral-rich foods. From bee pollen and maca to reishi and lion's mane, all of these superfoods offer unique healing properties and well-rounded nutritional support. I urge you to try the plant-based superfoods I've included in this book, but if your budget does not allow, please do not think that good health is not attainable for you. Eating plenty of fresh vegetables and fruits combined with whole grains and greens will always be good for you and the foundation of good health.

When stocking up your pantry with all these exciting products, start slow. You don't need to buy them all. Keep it simple. You also don't need five different superfoods in a smoothie – your body can't digest them all anyway. Read up about what they offer you and see which ones align with your needs. I have also designed most of the recipes so that the superfoods are an added optional benefit, so please don't let the lack of a superfood addition stop you from trying out the recipe.

SALT

A good-quality salt makes the flavours pop, which is why I only use Maldon salt to finish a dish off or Himalayan pink salt while cooking. These also contain more minerals than commercial salt and do not include any caking agents or chemicals. Check the back of the box or salt grinder when buying and, wherever possible, avoid salts that have caking agents or chemicals in them.

FRUITS AND VEGGIES

Wash your fruit, veggies and your greens. This is something that is so important when it comes to our food. Often, food has been sprayed with chemicals or pesticides and although we would love to live in a world or at least shop in a world of purely organic, it's not always possible. Washing your food is an important part of preparing it, not only to remove the bulk of these pesticides or any harmful bacteria or germs, but also to allow you to connect with what you are about to cook.

MILK ALTERNATIVES

As I have mentioned before I am not a big advocate for dairy milk. Why? Because the demand over the last century has grown exponentially and mass production and ethical free-range cannot go hand in hand. The result? Hormone- and antibiotic-riddled milk that is not good for your health. In nature, a cow only lactates when it is breastfeeding. In order for it to produce milk all the time for the dairy industry, it is impregnated and given hormones to increase the volume of supply. For that reason, in this book and always, I use milk alternatives. I go for the unsweetened and purest product I can afford and get my hands on at the time. Read your labels. Even almond milk can contain chemicals and have environmental impacts. That being said, I pick my battles and for me, dairy milk always loses.

If you do wish to use dairy milk and dairy products, then research local small-scale farmers who are doing it ethically and organically. Local farmers' markets are great places to find more ethical and wholesome meat and dairy products. Chat to the farmer and find out where your products are coming from.

SUGAR

Refined sugar is an empty calorie that will just spike your blood sugar and leave you with brain fog and false hunger.

I avoid it as often as I can. I also don't cook with it. When buying unrefined brown sugar be sure of its source. Big brands often use refined sugar tossed in caramel and then sell it as treacle sugar. Pure treacle sugar from sugar cane is unrefined and can form part of a balanced life when used in moderation. Coconut sugar is another glorious replacement for refined sugar and can add a uniquely sweet flavour to your dish. Do some research into the variety of sweetener options available and preferably buy natural replacements such as maple syrup or honey instead of options containing chemicals.

GHEE

Ghee is one of Ayurveda's most treasured foods and has many healing properties, including intestinal and skin health. I use it in place of butter or at the end of cooking to add some extra flavour. Whichever way you enjoy ghee, it is important to know a few things. Firstly, ghee is a dairy product and is, essentially, clarified butter. Secondly, you can make it yourself by gently heating butter until it separates into a translucent or clarified layer (the ghee) and solid sediment (the milk solids, which are discarded). Finally, even those who are lactose intolerant can enjoy this product as the casein and milk solids are removed during production. I usually find mine at the local health food store or at my local organic market. Where recipes call for ghee, vegans can use coconut oil or olive oil instead.

BREAD

Not all bread is created equal. When it comes to bread I support my local baker who uses stone-ground flour and bakes chemical-free loaves. Whether you enjoy rye or sourdough, as long as it has been created with unbleached flour and is naturally fermented, I say enjoy it in moderation. I opt for sourdough. As a fermented food it is alive with good microbes that support good gut health. It also freezes very well, which means you can slice it, freeze it and enjoy a crunchy slice of toast with some roasted tomatoes and avocado on it as a healthy snack, lunch or breakfast. Get creative with it. I've included several ideas for toast in this book as I have fallen in love with beautifully made bread along this journey to balanced health. Let's focus less on the carb fear and more on the complexity and health benefits from healthy carbs enjoyed with balance in mind.

APPLE CIDER VINEGAR

The only apple cider vinegar I use in this book is 100 per cent raw and unfiltered. It needs to come with the 'mother', which is its living good bacteria. This means that the health properties are intact. Once opened, store the bottle in the fridge and not in the cupboard.

HONEY

In this book, I use 100 per cent raw and sustainably sourced organic honey. If you are vegan, feel free to substitute it with maple syrup. I use honey because it has many health benefits that help to fight bad bacteria and combat inflammation. Avoid heating honey to a high temperature as this can damage the healing properties.

LIQUID AMINOS

You can use liquid aminos to add a beautiful salty flavour to a dish. If you can't find liquid aminos at your local health store, you can use tamari or soy sauce instead.

OLIVE OIL

Buying extra virgin cold pressed olive oil is best as all the healthy fats and nutrients are intact. Olive oil has a low smoke point so I usually use it for a slow low-temperature roast as well as raw on salads and in dressings. Avoid olive oils mixed with other oils – these may be more affordable, but the compromise is quality and health.

GRAINS, PULSES AND LEGUMES

I keep jars full of gorgeous grains, pulses and legumes in my pantry. I love them! They are brimming with vitamins and minerals, not to mention that they are high in protein and fibre, and you can add them to most dishes and salads. I try to avoid anything processed or bleached and opt for GMO-free.

When it comes to chickpeas, lentils and dried beans, soaking them overnight is best and can aid digestion. Once they are soaked, cook them as per the packet instructions in salted water.

I try to avoid tinned food whenever possible. Of course, the reality is that it isn't always possible to do so. We all lead busy lives and sometimes we forget to soak chickpeas overnight.

NUTS AND SEEDS

Nuts and seeds are a wonderful add-on to any meal. I love playing around with them for crunch and use them raw or roasted in salads, curries and breakfast porridges. When I roast the nuts, I either do so in a pan over medium heat or in the oven at 180 °C for 10–15 minutes.

Seeds can be toasted in a dry pan. Keep an eye on them as they can burn quickly so make sure to toss them regularly until they are golden brown and extra crunchy.

SMOOTHIES AND ELIXIRS

This chapter is here to get you thinking about breakfast and to look at how you choose to nourish yourself early in the morning. It is a chapter filled with light, fruity smoothies as well as creamier, dense smoothies for when you need that extra sustenance. I have also added some satisfying substitutes for coffee and tea that are wondrously healthy and can be enjoyed in place of that heavy caffeine dose so early in the morning. Don't get me wrong, coffee is neither good nor bad. It is simply about assessing your lifestyle and seeing whether or not the coffee you are drinking is adding stress to your adrenal glands or not. If you are already stressed and lacking sleep, ask yourself if coffee really is the solution or is it just a quick fix?

There are so many schools of thought out there about eating breakfast. Some come from the idea that breakfast is the most important meal of the day and others suggest intermittent fasting. The question to ask is, what really works for *you*? Forget about what you have been told. How do *you* feel when you wake up in the morning? Does it change day by day or from season to season?

For example, I cannot have a cold smoothie in winter. I find my digestion doesn't get going and further to that I simply don't crave them. I have a much better start to my day in winter when I have a warm, high-protein breakfast, be it chia porridge or crunchy avo toast. However, the second a hot summer morning arrives I am in full swing with smoothies. The light, cooling breakfast works for me and I enjoy how quick and easy they are. The bottom line? Are you eating when you wake up because you were told to or because you are hungry? Are you eating what you are eating because you have been led to believe that it is good for you or because that diet you read once upon a time said you should be eating bacon and eggs?

So, let's dive in. Here are three questions I want you to answer before you get into this chapter:

- What does a balanced breakfast look like to you?

- How do you experience your mornings?

- How busy is your day ahead and what type of whole food will nourish you best?

HEALTH TIPS
- Drink a glass of warm lemon water every morning. This will help fire up your digestive system as well as support good skin health.
- Taking a good-quality probiotic in the morning on an empty stomach will aid your gut microbiome and support gut healing.
- Chew, chew, chew your food. Doing so will break down larger particles, fire up your digestion and ready the body for the food to come. Chewing can also prevent overeating and is part of mindful eating.

CHOCOLATE EARTH

BEETROOT HOT CHOCOLATE WITH REISHI

SERVES: 2 | PREPARATION TIME: 20 MINUTES (*EXCLUDING STEAMING THE BEETROOT*)

Reishi is a medicinal mushroom that is used for treating cancer, slowing ageing, boosting the immune system, and to prevent or treat infections. It also supports good sleep and has a slightly bitter, earthy note to it, therefore pairing well with hot chocolate and coffees. Collagen supports good skin health, and there are both vegan and animal product derivatives, so find something that works well for your body. Collagen also aids in good joint health, relieving joint pain, and can boost muscle mass. Most importantly, it supports good gut health, which in turn can improve intestinal permeability and heal leaky gut.

1 MEDIUM-SIZED BEETROOT, STEAMED
  AND PEELED

1 CUP COCONUT MILK

3 TABLESPOONS RAW CACAO POWDER

1 TABLESPOON REISHI POWDER

2 TABLESPOONS MAPLE SYRUP

2 TEASPOONS VANILLA PASTE

2 TEASPOONS COLLAGEN
  POWDER (OPTIONAL)

Place all the ingredients into a blender and blend until smooth. Pour the liquid into a saucepan and bring to a simmer over low heat. Pour into mugs and serve, if desired, with a dusting of cacao powder and finely chopped dark chocolate.

FOREST SMOOTHIE

PASSION FRUIT AND GREENS

SERVES: 1 | PREPARATION TIME: 10 MINUTES

Broccoli is high in fibre and antioxidants, both of which support stomach function and digestive health, in turn treating symptoms of IBS (irritable bowel syndrome) and excess oestrogen which causes inflammation in the body. Eating fibre-rich food feeds good bacteria in the gut and this antioxidant and vitamin C-rich smoothie sets you up for a powerful day.

---

1 HANDFUL BABY SPINACH

4 TENDER-STEM BROCCOLI FLORETS

½ BANANA, PEELED AND FROZEN

1 CUP COCONUT WATER

1–3 TEASPOONS MACA POWDER

6 FRESH MINT LEAVES

2 MEDJOOL DATES, PITTED

PULP OF 2 PASSION FRUIT (GRANADILLAS)

2 KALE LEAVES, STALKS REMOVED

1 SERVING PLANT-BASED PROTEIN POWDER

½ TEASPOON GROUND TURMERIC

2 ICE CUBES (OPTIONAL)

ALMOND MILK (OPTIONAL)

Place all the ingredients, except the almond milk, into a blender and blend until smooth. Add almond milk if the consistency is too thick. Garnish with a dollop of passion fruit pulp, if desired.

LION'S MANE

HOT CHOCOLATE AND MUSHROOM

SERVES: 1 | PREPARATION TIME: 15 MINUTES

Lion's mane is a medicinal mushroom that can be bought in powder or capsule form at your local health store. It relieves symptoms of anxiety and depression, speeds up recovery from nervous system injuries and can help manage symptoms of diabetes. It is also a powerful anti-inflammatory for the body, which makes it an incredible immune support. Lion's mane is a healing food that falls under the superfood category.

- 1 TEASPOON LION'S MANE POWDER OR MUSHROOM SUPERFOOD POWDER
- 1 TABLESPOON MAPLE SYRUP
- 1 TABLESPOON RAW CACAO POWDER
- ½ TEASPOON GROUND CINNAMON
- SMALL PINCH OF SALT
- 1 CUP COCONUT MILK
- 1 SHOT ESPRESSO OR ⅓ CUP STRONG BREWED COFFEE (OPTIONAL)

Place all the ingredients, except the coffee, into a blender and blend until smooth. Transfer the liquid to a saucepan and stir in the coffee (if using). Bring to a simmer over low heat, simmer for 1 minute and then remove from the heat. Adjust the flavour, if needed, by adding more cinnamon, coffee or maple syrup. Pour into a mug and serve.

STRESS RELIEF LATTE

ADAPTOGEN POTION

SERVES: 1 | PREPARATION TIME: 15 MINUTES

Ashwagandha is a powerful adaptogen. An adaptogen, as the name suggests, is a herbal substance that helps the body adapt to stress and fatigue, and has been used for centuries in Chinese and Ayurvedic healing traditions. Ashwagandha is one of the incredible herbs that I have brought into my life and take daily because it helps manage adrenal fatigue and hormone imbalances which someone with PCOS (polycystic ovary syndrome), like myself, is likely to suffer from. Ashwagandha can also lower blood sugar levels, as well as fight symptoms of anxiety and depression, and can also boost fertility and testosterone levels in men. I don't recommend taking adaptogens on an empty stomach as they can make you feel nauseous.

- ½ CUP ALMOND MILK
- ½ CUP COCONUT MILK
- 3 MEDJOOL DATES, PITTED
- 1 TABLESPOON CASHEW NUT BUTTER
- 1 TABLESPOON MACA POWDER
- 1 TABLESPOON HEMP SEEDS FOR EXTRA PROTEIN (OPTIONAL)
- 1 TEASPOON VANILLA PASTE
- 1 TEASPOON COCONUT SUGAR (OPTIONAL)
- ½ TEASPOON ASHWAGANDHA POWDER

Place all the ingredients, except the ashwagandha powder, into a blender and blend until smooth. Transfer the liquid to a saucepan and bring to a simmer over low heat. Simmer for 1 minute, then remove from the heat and stir in the ashwagandha. If the latte is too thick, add some hot water to reach desired consistency. Garnish with hemp seeds, a dusting of maca powder or as otherwise desired.

FRESH START

CALMING MINT SMOOTHIE

SERVES: 1 | PREPARATION TIME: 10 MINUTES (*EXCLUDING STEAMING THE COURGETTES*)

Spirulina is a powerful anti-inflammatory and a fantastic source of antioxidants, which can protect against oxidative damage. Its main active component is phycocyanin, which gives spirulina its blue-green colour and fights free radicals in the body. Spirulina can lower bad LDL cholesterol and triglyceride levels. It also reduces blood pressure as it causes increased production of nitric oxide, a signalling molecule that helps blood vessels relax and dilate. Spirulina is readily available at most health stores and is something I recommend giving a try.

1 CUP ALMOND MILK

1 HANDFUL BABY SPINACH

1 SERVING PLANT-BASED PROTEIN POWDER

1 TEASPOON CHLORELLA OR SPIRULINA

½ CUP COURGETTE CHUNKS, STEAMED
   THEN FROZEN

1 KIWI FRUIT, PEELED

2 MEDJOOL DATES, PITTED

8 FRESH MINT LEAVES

2 ICE CUBES (OPTIONAL)

6 DROPS CBD OIL, OR DOSAGE AS
   RECOMMENDED BY YOUR HOMEOPATH
   OR PRODUCT

1 TABLESPOON CACAO NIBS

Place all the ingredients, except the cacao nibs, into a blender and blend until smooth. Add the cacao nibs and blend for 3 seconds (you want the nibs to be only slightly chopped up for that extra crunch). Garnish with a sprig of mint and a sprinkling of cacao nibs, if desired.

MORNING ZING

IMMUNE BOOSTER SMOOTHIE

SERVES: 1 | PREPARATION TIME: 10 MINUTES

Camu camu is incredibly rich in vitamin C and contains powerful antioxidants along with many other potent compounds which support a healthy immune system. It is native to the Amazon rainforest and comes from a berry that is very tart in flavour. It is considered a superfood due to its high content of powerful plant compounds. It also has antimicrobial properties and reduces potentially harmful bacteria in the body. Using it in a smoothie or salad dressing is a fun and easy way to make it palatable.

1 ORANGE, PEELED

1 TEASPOON CAMU CAMU POWDER

½ TEASPOON GROUND TURMERIC

½ THUMB-SIZE PIECE FRESH
   GINGER, PEELED

1 BANANA, PEELED AND FROZEN

1 CUP COCONUT WATER

1 TEASPOON COCONUT OIL

1 SERVING PLANT-BASED PROTEIN POWDER

2 ICE CUBES (OPTIONAL)

Place all the ingredients into a blender and blend until smooth. Garnish with a sprinkling of turmeric, if desired.

SMOOTHIE BAR

There are so many incredible smoothie combinations out there. At the end of the day it comes down to what works for your body. Play around with adding vegetables, such as steamed sweet potato instead of frozen banana, and see how you feel after having your smoothie. How long does it keep you full? I recommend adding a protein element as this will keep you fuller for longer. You can also add superfoods such as cacao or maca. Each one offers you a different health benefit to pack a powerful punch to the start of your day or even your midday meal!

CAULIFLOWER AND BLUEBERRY

- 2 TABLESPOONS ALMOND BUTTER
- 1 CUP CAULIFLOWER FLORETS, STEAMED THEN FROZEN
- ½ CUP FRESH OR FROZEN BLUEBERRIES
- 1 CUP ALMOND MILK
- 50 GRAMS RAW CASHEW NUTS
- ¼ FROZEN OR FRESH AVOCADO, PEELED AND PIP REMOVED
- ½ TEASPOON GROUND CINNAMON
- 2 MEDJOOL DATES, PITTED
- 2 ICE CUBES (OPTIONAL)

WHITE CHOCOLATE

- ⅓ CUP COOKED BUTTER BEANS
- 1 BANANA, PEELED AND FROZEN
- 1¼ CUPS ALMOND MILK
- 2 TABLESPOONS COCONUT BUTTER
- 1 TEASPOON CACAO BUTTER
- 1 TEASPOON VANILLA PASTE
- 1 TABLESPOON MAPLE SYRUP
- ½ TEASPOON GROUND CARDAMOM
- 1 TABLESPOON DRIED CRANBERRIES, PLUS EXTRA FOR SERVING
- 1 TABLESPOON CHIA SEEDS
- 5 RAW MACADAMIA NUTS, ROUGHLY CHOPPED, PLUS EXTRA FOR SERVING
- 2 ICE CUBES (OPTIONAL)

GINGER AND SPICE

- 1 BANANA, PEELED AND FROZEN
- 1 TABLESPOON MAPLE SYRUP OR 2 MEDJOOL DATES, PITTED
- 1 TEASPOON FINELY GRATED FRESH GINGER
- 1 TABLESPOON TAHINI
- 1 CUP ALMOND MILK (OR NUT MILK OF YOUR CHOICE)
- 3 TABLESPOONS ROLLED OATS
- ½ TEASPOON GROUND TURMERIC
- 1 ORANGE, PEELED
- 1 SERVING PLANT-BASED PROTEIN POWDER (OPTIONAL)
- 2 ICE CUBES (OPTIONAL)

BERRY

- ½ CUP FRESH OR FROZEN BLUEBERRIES
- 1 LARGE HANDFUL BABY SPINACH
- 1 BANANA, PEELED AND FROZEN
- 5 FRESH BASIL LEAVES
- 1 TABLESPOON ALMOND BUTTER
- 2 TABLESPOONS HEMP SEEDS OR 1 SERVING PLANT-BASED PROTEIN POWDER
- 1 CUP COCONUT WATER
- 2 TEASPOONS BEE POLLEN (OPTIONAL)
- 2 ICE CUBES (OPTIONAL)

PERSIMMON

- 1 BANANA, PEELED AND FROZEN
- 4 PERSIMMONS, HALVED
- 1 CUP COCONUT WATER
- 1 SMALL HANDFUL FRESH MINT LEAVES
- 1 TABLESPOON CHIA SEEDS
- 1 SERVING PLANT-BASED PROTEIN POWDER
- 2 ICE CUBES (OPTIONAL)

GREEN

- 1 GENEROUS HANDFUL BABY SPINACH
- 1 BANANA, PEELED AND FROZEN
- 1 TABLESPOON WHEAT GRASS OR BARLEY
- 1 SERVING PLANT-BASED PROTEIN
- 1 TABLESPOON CHIA SEEDS
- 1 CUP COCONUT WATER
- JUICE OF ½ LEMON
- 2 ICE CUBES (OPTIONAL)

For all these smoothies, place all the ingredients into a blender and blend until smooth. Garnish as desired with a sprinkling of one of the key ingredients used to make the smoothies.

BRUNCH

The reason I included a brunch chapter is simply because I want you to listen to your body. What time do you want to eat and what do you want to eat? Are you in the mood for a light, fruity breakfast or a decadent lunch at 11 am?

I also want you to start to look at the emotions that are driving your food choices and ask yourself, where do they come from? Bringing awareness around our food choices allows us to look a little deeper. To see that our emotional body drives our food choices can be a massive realisation. This is why so many of us are emotional eaters. Boredom, sadness, even joy which in turn leads to celebrations.

There is no wrong or right here – it's simply an opportunity to look inward and be mindful of our food choices, creating the possibility to change our choices because of self-awareness. The hard part is unpacking why we don't always make the best choices regardless of self-awareness. It's in this space that I ask you to be kind to yourself and to explore with an open heart and mind. Healthy eating takes time and the more you work towards it, the easier it becomes.

Healing our relationship with food starts with healing the relationship with ourselves and we do this by unpacking the past, sitting with the hard emotions that come up, processing them and healing our emotional wounds. This in turn supports us to make decisions based on self-love and little acts of kindness. Ultimately, healthy eating is a radical act of self-love and a representation of healing.

This chapter has something for everyone. So, tuck in, get lost in the music, cook your heart out and have fun creating healing food. If you are on the run during the week I have highlighted the recipes that are quicker and easier. If you find yourself with your music playing on a Sunday after you have slept in and you have more time to cook, then why not take on a longer recipe? Get into your kitchen flow and use cooking as a time to reflect and meditate on your life.

- What are the obstacles in your way that prevent you from making healthier food choices and embarking on a life-changing journey?

- What are your three most recurring emotions and how often do they drive your food choices?

- What will your life look like if you don't let emotions drive your food choice?

HEALTH TIPS
- Eat as much 'live' food as you can. By live, I mean fresh, real food. Not only is it packed with nutrients, but it also promotes good gut health because it is rich in fibre. Focus on as many colours of fresh fruit and vegetables as you can. Eat the rainbow!
- Move your body daily in a gentle and loving way. Whether it is a walk or yoga, movement is the key to *growing old* not *getting old*.
- Avoid processed sugars and read food labels. Dextrose and fructose are just other names for sugar and a clever way that companies like to hide sugar in their food. Even health products can be sneaky, so always read the labels. If you have sugar cravings, focus on eating naturally sweet foods such as apples or sweet potatoes.

SOURDOUGH

STARTER AND BREAD

MAKES: 1 LARGE LOAF | PREPARATION TIME: 5 DAYS FOR THE STARTER,
1 DAY FOR THE LOAF | BAKING TIME: 60 MINUTES

This is an incredible recipe that offers you a variety of options once you get the swing of it. Your obvious choice is to create utterly delicious sourdough bread or you can create a flatbread that can become a go-to snack. You can also elevate it and create a sourdough pizza base that can be adorned with a variety of colourful toppings. Eating sourdough means that you are eating a naturally fermented food. Fermented food is incredibly good for gut health. If you suffer indigestion after eating commercial store-bought bread, I encourage you to give this recipe a try as most people find that sourdough eradicates heartburn and offers all the comfort that you are looking for from bread.

SOURDOUGH STARTER

¾ CUP STONEGROUND BREAD FLOUR
½ CUP ROOM TEMPERATURE WATER
MUSLIN CLOTH OR CLEAN TEA TOWEL

LEAVEN

3 TABLESPOONS ACTIVE
   SOURDOUGH STARTER
½ CUP STONEGROUND BREAD FLOUR
⅓ CUP ROOM TEMPERATURE WATER

SOURDOUGH BREAD

2½ CUPS ROOM TEMPERATURE WATER
700 GRAMS STONEGROUND BREAD FLOUR
1½ TABLESPOONS SALT
½ CUP FLOUR FOR SPRINKLING

Making a sourdough starter takes 5 days. The reason for this is because the natural yeast grows stronger over this period and this is what you will use to make your bread rise. Over the 5-day period it will develop a sour smell, which is an indication of the natural fermentation. To make the initial starter, mix the flour and water together in a glass container that can accommodate up to a litre. The reason for this is because the starter will grow in size and you don't want it to overflow. You also need to have space to feed your starter daily with more flour. Once you have mixed the flour and water until well combined (you can use a fork) – the batter must be smooth and sticky – cover the starter with the muslin cloth or tea towel and set aside at a consistent room temperature for 24 hours.

You need to start feeding your starter on day 2 with a mixture of water and flour. This means you will repeat the process of adding and mixing in ¾ cup flour and ½ cup water. You will see bubbles developing in your starter and your starter will grow in volume.

To maintain your starter, make sure you feed it daily. You can also reduce the volume of your starter by using some to make the Sourdough Pancakes on page 165 or sharing it with a friend and then continuing to feed what is left.

After 5 days, your sourdough starter will be ready to make the leaven. Take 3 tablespoons of the active starter and combine it with the flour and water. Allow this mixture to sit and ferment overnight or for at least 12 hours at room temperature.

To make the bread, place the leaven in a large mixing bowl and add 2¼ cups of the water. Add the flour and mix with a fork until well combined and your dough is sticky. Let this mixture rest, covered with a tea towel, for 3–4 hours. During this stage the flour will absorb the water and enzymes in the flour will begin breaking down the starches and proteins.

After 4 hours, mix the salt into the remaining ¼ cup of water and stir until dissolved. Add this mixture to the dough by lightly working it in with your fingers. From this stage it is important to work gently with your bread using your hands. Don't knead the dough.

Every half hour for the next 2½ hours you will need to fold the dough in the bowl using your fingertips. You fold it by pinching the outside of the dough and pulling it towards you. Do this a minimum of 4 times per folding. The dough will be slightly puffed.

Place a clean dish cloth in a colander or deep bowl. Generously sprinkle the cloth with flour so that it is evenly covered with a layer of flour. Gently tip your dough out of the bowl into the colander. Set aside in a warm place in the kitchen (I stand mine next to my oven) for 40 minutes. Towards the end of this stage, preheat the oven to 200 °C.

Once the oven is hot, place a cast-iron or heavy-based pot with its lid into the oven for 15 minutes. Make sure the lid is ovenproof. This preheats the pot and supports the rising of the bread. Once the pot is hot, remove it from the oven and dust the bottom of the pot with flour. Gently tip your bread dough into the pot. If the dish cloth sticks to the dough then gently pinch it off.

Using a sharp knife, score the top of the loaf in a pattern of choice (you can even press some edible flowers into the top of the loaf, if you like). Pop the lid on the pot and bake in the oven for 40 minutes. After 40 minutes, remove the lid and bake for a further 15–20 minutes until the crust is golden brown and crispy.

Remove from the pot and set aside to cool on a wire rack.

GREEN WAFFLES

SWEET AND SAVOURY

MAKES: 5 WAFFLES | PREPARATION TIME: 35 MINUTES | COOKING TIME: 15 MINUTES

It's the weekend and the whole family wants a delicious breakfast. Here is the solution: these waffles with their hidden vegetables and delicious topping choices will make sure the whole family's needs are met. Let the children get involved with this one and pick their toppings. Fruit offers the sweetness craved by a young palate and is a much better start to the day than a sugary cereal devoid of nutrition.

1¼ CUPS ALMOND MILK OR MILK
  SUBSTITUTE OF YOUR CHOICE
1 HANDFUL BABY SPINACH
1 TEASPOON APPLE CIDER VINEGAR
¼ CUP OLIVE OR COCONUT OIL
⅓ CUP MAPLE SYRUP
½ CUP ROLLED OATS
1⅓ CUPS GLUTEN-FREE FLOUR
1½ TEASPOONS BAKING POWDER
PINCH OF SALT

WHIPPED COCONUT CREAM

½ CUP COCONUT CREAM SOLID (SEE
  PAGE 189)
1 TEASPOON VANILLA PASTE
1 TABLESPOON MAPLE SYRUP (OR
  XYLITOL IF YOU WANT THE CREAM TO
  STAY WHITE)
¼ TEASPOON AGAR AGAR POWDER

TOPPING OPTION 1

FRIED EGGS
NUTRITIONAL YEAST FOR SPRINKLING
FRESH LEMON JUICE
MICRO HERBS AND SALAD LEAVES
SALT AND PEPPER

TOPPING OPTION 2

FRESH BERRIES
MAPLE SYRUP
DARK CHOCOLATE CHIPS
SLICED BANANA (OPTIONAL)
GROUND CINNAMON FOR SPRINKLING
WHIPPED COCONUT CREAM (SEE ABOVE)

Heat your waffle iron to medium heat. Each iron is different so you will need to do a test waffle to make sure it cooks through.

Place the milk and spinach into a high-speed blender and blend until smooth. Transfer to a large mixing bowl and stir in the apple cider vinegar. Let this sit for 10 minutes until it starts to curdle. Add the oil and maple syrup, whisk and set aside.

Place the oats, flour, baking powder and salt into a large bowl and whisk until mixed. Add the wet ingredients to the dry ingredients and mix until well combined, making sure there are no lumps. The mixture should be thick enough to scoop. Let the batter sit for 5–10 minutes.

For the whipped coconut cream, place the solid coconut cream into a stand mixer with the whisk attachment and whisk on high speed. Once stiff peaks start to form, add the remaining ingredients and whisk until well combined. Cover the bowl and pop it into the fridge for 20 minutes.

Preheat the oven to 200 °C.

Lightly grease the waffle iron. I use coconut oil and a paper towel to wipe it down and lightly coat it, but you can also use a brush. Pour ½ cup batter into the iron. I cook the waffles slightly longer than the manufacturers' recommendations as this is a gluten-free batter which needs a little more heat.

Once ready, keep the waffles warm in the oven while you make the rest. I don't stack them, but rather place them separately so that they stay crisp on the outside. Don't leave them in there too long as they will dry out.

Once all the waffles are ready, serve them immediately with the suggested toppings (or your own choice of healthy toppings), letting your little ones decorate their own waffles and connect with their food!

CHOCOLATE QUINOA

NUTTY PORRIDGE

SERVES: 4 | PREPARATION TIME: 10 MINUTES | COOKING TIME: 35 MINUTES

Having an attitude of gratitude can go a long way in life. Waking up every morning and writing down five things you are grateful for can support mental and emotional health. It supports anxiety and depression, which in turn helps fight off stress. Take a moment when making this recipe, or perhaps when you are tasting it, to be grateful. It's delicious and indulgent and sparks joy.

2 TEASPOONS COCONUT OIL

1 CUP UNCOOKED QUINOA

2 CUPS BOILING WATER

SALT

1 CUP ALMOND MILK

1 BANANA, SLICED, PLUS EXTRA FOR
    SERVING (OPTIONAL)

½ TEASPOON GROUND CINNAMON

1 TABLESPOON RAW CACAO POWDER
    OR 50 GRAMS DARK CHOCOLATE OF
    YOUR CHOICE

2 TABLESPOONS ALMOND BUTTER

80 GRAMS FRESH BLUEBERRIES

2 TEASPOONS HONEY

Place the coconut oil into a medium-sized saucepan over medium heat. Add the quinoa and stir, allowing it to toast for roughly 2 minutes. Add the boiling water and a good crack of salt, and bring to a simmer for 15–20 minutes. As the last bit of water is absorbed in the saucepan, switch off the heat, cover with a lid and allow the quinoa to steam for 5 minutes. You can either make this the night before and store in an airtight container or continue cooking.

Add the almond milk, 1 banana and the cinnamon to the quinoa and simmer over medium heat for 15 minutes. About 5 minutes before the quinoa porridge is ready, add the cacao or chocolate and fold through.

Spoon into bowls, top with almond butter and serve with fresh blueberries, a lick of honey, extra sliced banana (if using) and edible flowers.

VARIATION
Fry the remaining banana in 2 teaspoons coconut oil for around 10 minutes over medium heat until caramelised.

MORNING CRUNCH

GINGER AND LIME GRANOLA

MAKES: 1 LARGE GLASS JAR (ROUGHLY 800 GRAMS) | PREPARATION TIME: 15 MINUTES
COOKING TIME: 30 MINUTES

This recipe is high in fibre, packed with flavour and has the ultimate crunch to it. It can be made ahead and stored in an airtight container. This will make mornings a little easier and also provide you with a healthy snack when you need it. Setting up your breakfast routine for success is so important in finding balance each morning.

⅓ CUP TAHINI
½ CUP MAPLE SYRUP
2½ TABLESPOONS GROUND GINGER
⅓ CUP COCONUT OIL
1 CUP RAW ALMONDS
½ CUP PUMPKIN SEEDS
¼ CUP CHIA SEEDS
1 TABLESPOON GROUND FLAX SEEDS
¼ CUP SUNFLOWER SEEDS
⅓ CUP BUCKWHEAT
½ CUP COCONUT FLAKES
ZEST OF 3 LIMES
½ TEASPOON SALT
⅓ CUP GOJI BERRIES

Preheat the oven to 160 °C. Line a baking tray with baking paper.

In a small bowl, combine the tahini, maple syrup, ginger and coconut oil and whisk together.

In a large bowl, combine the almonds, seeds, buckwheat, coconut flakes, lime zest and salt. Add the tahini mixture and fold through until combined.

Tip the granola mix onto the prepared baking tray and spread it out evenly. Bake for 20 minutes at 160 °C until the mixture starts to become golden brown. After 20 minutes gently toss the granola then reduce the heat to 120 °C for a further 10 minutes. Once ready, remove from the oven and add the goji berries. Mix until well combined.

Allow the mixture to cool and then store in an airtight container.

You can top smoothie bowls with the mixture, have it as a snack or enjoy it as a cereal with some nut milk.

HEARTY FRITTATA

POTATO AND ARTICHOKE

SERVES: 6 | PREPARATION TIME: 15 MINUTES | COOKING TIME: 35 MINUTES

When it comes to fresh produce I make the effort to buy food that isn't wrapped in plastic. So many food items don't need to be wrapped at all, or they are put into a plastic bag when weighed and then into another when paid for. I want you to think about what type of consumer you want to be. Do you want to be someone who only thinks of the short term and 'self' or someone that thinks of the collective 'we' on a global level? It may seem like your actions don't make a difference, but they do. Supporting plastic-free grocery stores or buying 'conscious' products helps small-scale sustainable businesses survive and hopefully thrive in the future. Shop at your local farmers' market or find a local fresh fruit and vegetable delivery service. Not only are you making a difference to the company and the planet, but you are shopping for healthier fresh food for yourself and family.

---

12 EGGS

PINCH OF SALT

¼ CUP FRESH DILL LEAVES, ROUGHLY
   CHOPPED

½ TEASPOON CAYENNE PEPPER

2 TEASPOONS COCONUT OIL

1 TEASPOON DRIED OREGANO

1 CUP PORCINI MUSHROOMS, SLICED

5 BABY POTATOES, SCRUBBED, BOILED,
   CUBED AND SET ASIDE TO COOL

½ CUP COOKED ARTICHOKE

2 HANDFULS BABY SPINACH

80 GRAMS RICOTTA CHEESE

OLIVE OIL

1 HANDFUL MICRO HERBS

Preheat the oven to 180 °C.

Whisk the eggs, salt, dill and cayenne pepper together in a large bowl until well combined. Set aside.

Heat the coconut oil in a large ovenproof frying pan over medium to high heat. Add the oregano and mushrooms and fry for 4 minutes or until the mushrooms begin to turn golden brown. Add the potatoes and artichoke and fry for a further 5 minutes. Once the vegetables are golden brown, lower the heat to medium and pour in the egg mixture. Stir the mixture until the eggs are slightly cooked at the bottom – sort of a gentle scramble if you will. Stop stirring and allow the eggs to cook halfway.

At this stage, add the baby spinach and dollops of ricotta cheese to cover the spinach, gently pressing it into the semi-cooked egg mixture using a spatula.

Remove the pan from the heat and pop it into the oven. Bake the frittata in the oven for 30–35 minutes or until the egg mixture is fully cooked.

Remove from the oven and drizzle over some olive oil. Top with micro herbs and season to taste.

BUCKWHEAT CRÊPES

SALTED CARAMEL AND GRANOLA

SERVES: 4 | PREPARATION TIME: 1 HOUR | COOKING TIME: 20 MINUTES

Bee pollen are pellets of gathered flower pollen. Bee pollen is an incredibly powerful food that needs to be sourced ethically from a small-scale local honey supplier. Ask around at your local farmers' market or health store to find some. Bee pollen fights inflammation, boosts liver health, strengthens the immune system and is a powerful antioxidant. Use it in moderation with respect to where it comes from.

CRÊPE MIXTURE

300 GRAMS BUCKWHEAT FLOUR
700 MILLILITRES WATER, PLUS EXTRA
COCONUT OIL

SALTED CARAMEL TAHINI SAUCE

2 TABLESPOONS TAHINI
2 TABLESPOONS MAPLE SYRUP
1 TEASPOON WATER
PINCH OF SALT

TO SERVE

GINGER AND LIME GRANOLA (SEE PAGE 48)
FRESH BLUEBERRIES
COCONUT YOGHURT OR A DAIRY YOGHURT
    OF YOUR CHOICE
BEE POLLEN (OPTIONAL AND ETHICALLY
    SOURCED)

For the crêpes, place the buckwheat flour and water in a large mixing bowl and whisk until well combined with no lumps. Set aside to rest for 1 hour. After 1 hour it will be thick, so add a little more water as needed to obtain a pancake batter consistency. The batter must be pourable but not watery.

In a small bowl, combine all the tahini sauce ingredients and set aside.

To cook the crêpes, add 1 teaspoon coconut oil to a medium-sized frying pan over medium heat. Pour in ½ cup of the crêpe mixture (depending on the size of your pan,) then tilt and swirl the pan so that the base is evenly covered. Cook for 40 seconds on each side or until you start to see bubbles round the edges. Once ready, remove from the pan and stack on a plate until ready to serve. Repeat with the remaining batter.

Once you have prepared all the crêpes, serve them with granola, caramel tahini sauce, blueberries, a dollop of yoghurt and a sprinkle of bee pollen (if using). Garnish with mint and edible flowers, if desired.

GREEN EGGS

SHAKSHUKA

SERVES: **2** | PREPARATION TIME: **15** MINUTES | COOKING TIME: **30** MINUTES

Making your kitchen a happy space means that not only do you get to enjoy it, but so do others who share the space with you. Spending time together in the kitchen is spending time together in the present, which is a beautiful gift that you can give your relationships. Even if you don't have somebody that you share your kitchen space with, you are creating time to be present with yourself. This is why cooking is a form of meditation for me.

---

2 TEASPOONS COCONUT OIL

1 LARGE LEEK, WASHED AND SLICED

1 CLOVE GARLIC, MINCED

1 GREEN CHILLI, FINELY SLICED

1 TEASPOON DRIED OREGANO

1 TEASPOON GROUND CUMIN

1 TEASPOON GROUND CORIANDER

100 GRAMS CHICKPEAS, COOKED (SEE
    PAGE 24)

100 GRAMS FRESH OR FROZEN PEAS

1 BUNCH TUSCAN KALE, STALKS REMOVED
    AND ROUGHLY CHOPPED

1 BUNCH SWISS CHARD, STALKS REMOVED
    AND ROUGHLY CHOPPED

4 EGGS

100 GRAMS RICOTTA CHEESE

1 SMALL HANDFUL FRESH MINT LEAVES,
    FINELY CHOPPED

1 SMALL HANDFUL FRESH DILL LEAVES,
    FINELY CHOPPED

ZEST AND JUICE OF 1 LEMON

OLIVE OIL

SALT AND PEPPER

Heat the coconut oil in a medium-sized frying pan over medium heat. Once hot, add the leek, garlic and chilli. Fry for 5 minutes until the leek starts to soften. Add the oregano, cumin and coriander and fry for a further 5 minutes. Add the chickpeas and peas and cook for another 5 minutes.

Stir in the kale and Swiss chard, letting the heat wilt the leaves for 3–5 minutes.

Using the back of a wooden spoon, create holes in the frying pan mixture. Break the eggs into the holes and cook for 6–8 minutes. Meanwhile, add dollops of ricotta in between the eggs.

In a bowl, combine the mint and dill. Once the eggs are cooked, remove the pan from the heat and season the shakshuka with lemon zest, a squeeze of lemon juice, a drizzle of olive oil and a crack of salt and pepper. Top with the mint and dill and serve.

POTATO RÖSTI

POACHED EGGS AND QUICK CUCUMBER PICKLE

SERVES: 2 | PREPARATION TIME: 15 MINUTES | COOKING TIME: 20 MINUTES

This is a dish to share with family, in whatever capacity that is for you. Having a healthier relationship with food and ourselves brings awareness to our relationships with family members. So often, our food stories of shame and guilt stem from a relationship dynamic in the space of our home. Moving into that emotional space with self-awareness and compassion allows us the opportunity to heal family relationships.

400 GRAMS CHERRY TOMATOES

COCONUT OIL

3 TABLESPOONS BALSAMIC VINEGAR

SALT AND PEPPER

4 MEDIUM-SIZED POTATOES, PEELED
    AND GRATED

3 EGGS

½ RED ONION, DICED

1 TABLESPOON GLUTEN-FREE FLOUR

1 TABLESPOON FRESH THYME LEAVES

¼ TEASPOON GROUND CUMIN

¼ TEASPOON GROUND TURMERIC

¼ TEASPOON CAYENNE PEPPER (OPTIONAL)

½ TABLESPOON WHITE VINEGAR

1 AVOCADO, PEELED AND PIP REMOVED

ZEST AND JUICE OF ½ LEMON

QUICK CUCUMBER PICKLE

½ CUCUMBER, PEELED AND THINLY SLICED
    INTO DISCS

1 TEASPOON CORIANDER SEEDS, BASHED
    WITH A MORTAR AND PESTLE

1 TEASPOON MAPLE SYRUP

ZEST AND JUICE 1 LEMON

1 TABLESPOON WHITE WINE VINEGAR

Preheat the oven to 180 °C.

Make the pickle first: place all the ingredients into a small bowl and mix well using your hands. Crush the cucumber lightly to get the flavours going. Store in a sterilised glass jar in the fridge – it will keep for up to a week.

Place the tomatoes, 1 tablespoon coconut oil and the balsamic vinegar in a roasting pan. Toss the tomatoes until evenly covered. Season with salt and pepper and pop them into the oven to roast for 35 minutes, tossing them at the halfway mark.

Meanwhile, place the potatoes, 1 egg, the onion, flour, thyme and spices in a large mixing bowl. Mix well and season with salt and pepper. Set aside.

Heat 2 teaspoons coconut oil in a medium-sized frying pan over medium heat. You are going to make 2 medium-sized röstis or 1 large one. The first step is to take the potato mixture in your hands and squeeze out the excess liquid. Once you have removed the excess liquid, place the potato mixture into the frying pan and shape into 2 medium-sized discs or 1 large disc roughly 1 cm thick. Fry the rösti for about 10 minutes until the bottom becomes crispy. Using a large spatula, gently flip the rösti over and fry for an additional 10 minutes.

Meanwhile, bring water to a simmer in a saucepan and add the vinegar. Swirl the water and then crack an egg into it (poach the eggs one at a time). Cook for 4–5 minutes and then remove using a slotted spoon. If you don't want to poach your eggs, do them the way you prefer.

When the tomatoes are ready, remove them from the oven.

Slice the avocado and get ready to serve the rösti. I like to layer it up by starting with my rösti, then adding my gooey tomatoes, topping with the egg and avocado then finishing off with a tablespoon of pickle. Sprinkle over the lemon zest and add a light drizzle of lemon juice. Top off with a crack of black pepper and garnish with micro herbs, if desired.

CHEESY QUICHE

ROASTED BUTTERNUT AND RICOTTA

SERVES: 4 | PREPARATION TIME: 15 MINUTES | COOKING TIME: 45 MINUTES

Looking after your energy means one simple thing: you will have more energy to do things you need and want to do. Real food provides energy. Exercise becomes easier and work becomes more manageable. Healing your energy by eating healthier means being aware of what you eat and cutting out refined sugars and processed foods. Make sure you get adequate sleep and allow yourself down time when you are exhausted. Operating from a place of exhaustion will mean that you are operating from a deficit – wouldn't you rather want to create a life from a place of vigour and zest? Your energy is finite and precious, and you should try to treat it as such – don't deplete it on extra hours at the office or on people who actually drain it.

CRUST

- 250 GRAMS SPELT FLOUR
- 1 TABLESPOON FRESH THYME LEAVES
- ¼ TEASPOON SALT
- ZEST OF 1 LEMON
- 6 TABLESPOONS OLIVE OIL
- ⅓ CUP COLD WATER

FILLING

- 300 GRAMS BUTTERNUT, PEELED AND CUT INTO SMALL PIECES
- 3 TEASPOONS COCONUT OIL
- SALT AND PEPPER
- 1 RED ONION, FINELY SLICED
- ¼ CUP BALSAMIC VINEGAR
- 1 HANDFUL KALE, STALKS REMOVED AND LEAVES TORN INTO BITE-SIZE PIECES
- 1 TABLESPOON FRESH THYME LEAVES
- 1 TEASPOON CHILLI FLAKES
- ½ TEASPOON CUMIN SEEDS
- 2 TABLESPOONS NUTRITIONAL YEAST
- 6 EGGS, BEATEN
- 100 GRAMS RICOTTA CHEESE

Preheat the oven to 180 °C. Grease a 24 cm pie dish.

To make the crust, combine the flour, thyme, salt and lemon zest in a food processor. Pulse until combined. Add the olive oil and pulse until crumbs form. Add the water slowly while blending until it combines into a ball of dough. (You can do this all by hand if need be.)

Roll out the dough on a floured surface to about 3 mm thick. If the dough starts separating while you're rolling, add a little more water, form it back into a ball and try again. Lift the dough onto the rolling pin and unroll it into the prepared pie dish. Gently press it into the sides. Prick the crust using a fork. Place a sheet of baking paper on top of the crust and top with uncooked rice or baking beans. Bake for 20–25 minutes until golden brown. Once ready, remove from the oven and set aside while you make the filling (keep the oven switched on).

Meanwhile, place the butternut onto a roasting tray and toss with 2 teaspoons of the coconut oil. Season with salt and pepper and then roast in the oven for 25–30 minutes. Once ready, transfer to a large mixing bowl and set aside.

Heat the remaining teaspoon of coconut oil in a small frying pan over medium heat and add the red onion. Sauté for 5 minutes until translucent, then add the balsamic vinegar and continue sautéing until the balsamic has reduced and the onion is caramelised.

Add the onion and remaining filling ingredients, except the ricotta, to the butternut and mix until well combined. Pour the filling into the crust. Crumble the ricotta evenly on top of the filling, but don't make the pieces too small. Pop the quiche into the oven to bake for 45 minutes. You know it is ready when the egg has set and cooked through.

Allow to cool slightly before serving with a fresh green salad and garnish of micro herbs of choice.

A NEW WAY TO SALAD

Salads are so much more than what you may initially think they are. Pushing the flavours and creating dynamic salads can truly open up a whole world of healthy eating. And the best thing is they can open the door to eating dark leafy greens.

Your body experiences the most incredible effects if you eat dark leafy greens. They are the king of alkalisation and they feed your telomeres. Telomeres are the little caps on our DNA chromosomes that protect our genetic data and are a big indicator of longevity. They hold the secrets to how the body ages and how cancer arises. Studies are now showing that the way we eat can switch genes on and off like a light switch. To fuel our telomeres, we have to eat what our cells eat to stay healthy, and dark leafy greens contain a lot of the components that our cells need.

When cooked correctly, dark leafy greens add beautiful complexity to a dish. Herbs such as parsley, basil and coriander are incredible flavour bombs, but there is such a large variety of flavours when it comes to greens that you should explore them and find what works for you. When it comes to salad ingredients, there is a vast array of beautiful produce and options – salads don't have to be cold bowls with only a few standard fresh ingredients. Explore the recipes in this chapter for some interesting new takes on salad.

- What resistance might you get from family and friends by making healthier food choices?

- What could you do differently in your food choices that is more loving towards your health?

- What thoughts and behaviours do you need to let go of in order to find more balance in your life?

HEALTH TIPS

- If you suffer from bloating, try incorporating these into your diet to soothe your stomach: peppermint tea, ginger tea, a tablespoon of apple cider vinegar in a glass of water, and try getting your hands on a good-quality digestive enzyme (you can find them at your local health store) to take before meals. Digestive enzymes are a group of enzymes that break down macronutrients and facilitate the absorption of nutrients into the body.
- Focus on eating foods that support good liver health. If your liver is not functioning optimally it can affect sleep, hormonal balance and toxin elimination. Eating a variety of vegetables and following an 80/20 rule with alcohol, caffeine, dairy, sugar and gluten will support liver health. The 80/20 rule is where you mindfully enjoy food and eat healthily for 80 per cent of the time, and allow for indulgences and life happening (such as cake and champagne at a birthday party) for the remaining 20 per cent. I also suggest taking milk thistle to support liver function.

ISLAND SALAD

GRILLED NECTARINES AND COCONUT

SERVES: 4 | PREPARATION TIME: 10 MINUTES | COOKING TIME: 25 MINUTES

Sweet is without a doubt one of the yummiest flavours and when contrasted with dark leafy greens, they can seem bitter and inedible. However, this is only true when it comes to refined sugars which plague so many people's day-to-day diets. Mixing different tastes such as sweet and bitter is how you can achieve real flavour; it's this contrast that makes a dish stand out. In this recipe, for example, I combine natural sugar from a fruit with the bitter greens which complements them beautifully and makes them incredibly enjoyable. So, if bitter greens aren't something you would typically eat, I encourage you to try this salad and experience how the flavours play off each other.

2 TEASPOONS COCONUT OIL

1 CUP UNCOOKED QUINOA (PREFERABLY RED)

4 CUPS BOILING WATER

SALT AND PEPPER

½ CUP EDAMAME BEANS, SHELLED

2 NECTARINES, HALVED AND PIPS REMOVED

OLIVE OIL

¼ CUP COCONUT FLAKES

50 GRAMS RAW MACADAMIA NUTS

2 HANDFULS BABY SPINACH

1 AVOCADO, PEELED, PIP REMOVED, CUBED

DRESSING

ZEST AND JUICE OF 2 LIMES

5 TABLESPOONS OLIVE OIL

1 TEASPOON HONEY

½ TEASPOON RED CHILLI FLAKES (OPTIONAL)

1 SMALL HANDFUL FRESH MINT LEAVES, FINELY CHOPPED

SALT AND PEPPER

Heat the coconut oil in a medium-sized saucepan over medium heat. Add the quinoa and stir, allowing the quinoa to toast for roughly 2 minutes. Add 2 cups of the boiling water and a good crack of salt, and bring to a simmer for 15–20 minutes. As the last of the water is absorbed in the saucepan, switch off the heat and cover with a lid, allowing the quinoa to steam for 5 minutes. Once steamed, remove the lid and spread out the quinoa on a baking tray, allowing it to cool.

Mix all the ingredients for the salad dressing together in a small bowl and season to taste. Set aside.

Place the shelled edamame beans in another small bowl and cover with the remaining 2 cups of boiling water. Blanch for 5 minutes and then rinse with cold water, drain and set aside.

Slice the nectarines into crescent shapes about 5 mm thick. Drizzle lightly with olive oil.

Heat a griddle pan over medium to high heat, then add the nectarines to the hot pan. Grill for 4–5 minutes on each side until grill marks appear. Remove from the heat and set aside.

Toast the coconut flakes in a small frying pan for 5 minutes until golden brown. Keep an eye on them so that they don't burn. Meanwhile, roughly chop the macadamia nuts.

Spread the spinach leaves over a medium-sized serving platter. Cover the spinach with the cooled quinoa and add the edamame beans. Top the salad with the avocado, nectarine slices, toasted coconut and macadamia nuts. Drizzle the dressing generously over the salad and season to taste with salt and pepper.

GARDEN HAUL

ROASTED TOMATOES AND CHICKPEAS

SERVES: 4 | PREPARATION TIME: 15 MINUTES | COOKING TIME: 45 MINUTES

In terms of Ayurveda, brown rice was recommended to work for my digestive system, and as I delved in I learnt it did. I feel satisfied after eating this dish because adding rice to a salad can make a meal that is often associated with light or small portions more substantial. Play around with different grains and pair them with fresh ingredients for a more dynamic and hearty salad.

250 GRAMS CHICKPEAS, COOKED (SEE PAGE 24)

300 GRAMS COURGETTES, CUT INTO 2 CM PIECES

400 GRAMS CHERRY TOMATOES

1 TABLESPOON COCONUT OIL

½ TEASPOON GROUND TURMERIC

½ TEASPOON CAYENNE PEPPER

SALT AND PEPPER

1 CUP UNCOOKED WILD BROWN RICE

2 HANDFULS ROCKET

1 TABLESPOON NUTRITIONAL YEAST

1 RIPE AVOCADO, PEELED, PIP REMOVED, SLICED

1 TABLESPOON BUCKWHEAT

1 TABLESPOON PUMPKIN SEEDS

DRESSING

¼ CUP OLIVE OIL

1 TABLESPOON TAHINI

1 TEASPOON HONEY

JUICE OF 1 MEDIUM-SIZED LEMON

Preheat the oven to 180 °C.

Place the chickpeas, courgettes and cherry tomatoes into a large roasting tray and coat them with the coconut oil. Add the turmeric and cayenne pepper and toss until evenly covered. Season and pop into the oven for 35–45 minutes or until all the veggies are golden brown and soft. Keep an eye on them so that the chickpeas don't burn and toss the veggies at the halfway point.

Cook the wild rice as per the packet instructions. Once ready, set aside.

Meanwhile, whisk all the dressing ingredients together in a small bowl.

Once the veggies are ready, remove them from the oven. Add the wild rice to the roasting tray along with the dressing, rocket and nutritional yeast. Mix together until well combined.

Transfer the salad to your serving dish. Top with the avo and sprinkle over the buckwheat and pumpkin seeds. Serve immediately.

TOSSED

TWO WAYS TO AN EASY GREEN SALAD

SERVES: 2 | PREPARATION TIME: 25 MINUTES

Paying attention to what your body needs on a physical and energetic level allows you to tune into the energy on offer in certain types of food. Eating a light green salad offers Vata dosha (see page 9) to the digestive system and body, as salad is seen as vata in ayurveda. Eating your greens can help balance the digestive system and your dosha energetically. So if you are feeling sluggish a light green salad can help increase energy levels and help get you moving for a walk or that exercise class.

ONE

100 GRAMS TENDER-STEM BROCCOLI
½ CUP FROZEN OR FRESH PEAS
1 HANDFUL BABY SPINACH
1 HANDFUL ROCKET
1 SMALL FENNEL BULB, STALKS AND
    LEAVES REMOVED, BULB THINLY SLICED
1 GREEN APPLE, CORED AND DICED
1 AVOCADO, PEELED, PIP REMOVED,
    CUBED
OLIVE OIL
JUICE OF ½ LEMON
50 GRAMS RAW WALNUTS, CHOPPED
SALT AND PEPPER

ONE

Place the broccoli and peas into a bowl of just-boiled water and blanch for 5–7 minutes. Rinse with cold water, drain and set aside.

Place the baby spinach, rocket, fennel and apple into a serving bowl. Add the avocado, some olive oil and the lemon juice and toss for a few minutes until the leaves are evenly coated.

Top with the walnuts, season to taste and serve with a garnish of choice.

TWO

1 HEAD COS LETTUCE, ROUGHLY CHOPPED
1 SMALL HANDFUL FRESH MINT
    LEAVES, CHOPPED
1 SMALL HANDFUL FRESH BASIL
    LEAVES, CHOPPED
1 SMALL HANDFUL FRESH DILL
    LEAVES, CHOPPED
½ LARGE CUCUMBER, DICED
1 AVOCADO, PEELED, PIP REMOVED,
    CUBED
½ WHEEL FETA CHEESE, CRUMBLED
    (OPTIONAL)
1 HANDFUL MIXED SPROUTS, ROUGHLY
    SEPARATED (ALFAFA, BEAN, CHICKPEA
    AND/OR BEETROOT)
JUICE AND ZEST OF ½ LEMON
GOOD DASH OF OLIVE OIL
SALT AND PEPPER

TWO

Place all the ingredients together in a bowl and toss until combined. Season to taste and serve with a garnish of choice.

AUTUMN LEAVES

SMOKY VEGETABLE SALAD

SERVES: 2 | PREPARATION TIME: 15 MINUTES | COOKING TIME: ±45 MINUTES

When you create delicious food for someone else, it sparks joy as it's like giving someone a present and watching their face light up. There is no greater gift than beautifully made, flavourful food.

---

1 HEAD CAULIFLOWER, BROKEN
   INTO FLORETS
COCONUT OIL
½ TABLESPOON SMOKED PAPRIKA
SALT AND PEPPER
250 GRAMS CHICKPEAS, COOKED (SEE
   PAGE 24)
400 GRAMS CHERRY TOMATOES
½ TEASPOON CAYENNE PEPPER
1 CUP UNCOOKED RED OR BROWN RICE
2¼ CUPS BOILING WATER
1 LARGE LEEK
1 RED PEPPER, SEEDED AND SLICED
1 YELLOW PEPPER, SEEDED AND SLICED
1 HANDFUL BABY SPINACH
80 GRAMS RAW ALMONDS, ROASTED (SEE
   PAGE 24)
1 AVOCADO, PEELED, PIP REMOVED,
   CUBED (OPTIONAL)

DRESSING

5 TABLESPOONS OLIVE OIL
2 TABLESPOONS TAHINI
JUICE OF 1 LEMON
1 TEASPOON HONEY
1 TABLESPOON WATER
SALT AND PEPPER

Preheat the oven to 180 °C.

Combine all the ingredients for the dressing in a small bowl and whisk together. Season to taste. If your dressing is a little bit thick, add an extra tablespoon of olive oil and give it a whisk. Set aside.

Place the cauliflower florets and 1 tablespoon coconut oil on a roasting tray. Add the smoked paprika and toss until the cauliflower is evenly coated. Season with salt and pepper.

Place the chickpeas and tomatoes on a separate roasting tray. Add 2 teaspoons coconut oil and the cayenne pepper, toss until evenly coated and season with salt and pepper.

Place both roasting trays into the oven and roast for 35–45 minutes, tossing the ingredients at the halfway mark. Keep an eye on the cauliflower as it may be ready sooner. You want the tomatoes to be gooey and soft.

Place the uncooked rice and 1 tablespoon coconut oil into a medium-sized saucepan over medium heat. Toast the rice for 2–5 minutes. Add the boiling water and a crack of salt and let it simmer for 30–35 minutes. Once the water has cooked off, switch off the heat and cover with a lid, allowing the rice to steam for 10 minutes.

Meanwhile, bring a large saucepan of water to a boil. Remove the outer leaves of the leek and wash the leek well. Slice the leek lengthways, stopping before the root end so it stays intact. Pop the leek into the water and cook for 5 minutes. Remove and drain.

Place a griddle pan over medium heat until it is hot. Lightly oil the leek with a little melted coconut oil and add it to the griddle pan. Grill for 5–10 minutes, turning at the halfway mark, until grill marks appear. Once ready, set aside on a chopping board to cool.

In a bowl, toss the peppers in a little melted coconut oil and add to the same griddle pan. Grill for 5–10 minutes until they are evenly grilled.

Once the rice is ready, transfer it to a salad bowl and fluff out using a fork. Allow to cool for 5 minutes. Slice the leek and add it to the rice. Add the spinach leaves and peppers and toss well. Add the cauliflower and top with the tomatoes and chickpeas. Drizzle over the dressing and toss again until combined. Sprinkle the almonds over the salad for extra crunch and top with the avocado (if using). Season to taste.

FOREST FLOOR

MUSHROOM AND PEARL BARLEY SALAD

SERVES: 2 | PREPARATION TIME: 10 MINUTES | COOKING TIME: 35 MINUTES

Fennel is a prime example of how food can heal. Fennel tea can support digestion, and cooking with it can ease bloating and support good gut health. It is a powerful green that can add a subtle anise flavour or the perfect crunch to a salad – if you aren't used to cooking with fennel, use only the bulb, not the leaves, for this recipe.

2½ CUPS WATER

SALT AND PEPPER

1 CUP PEARL BARLEY

350 GRAMS PORTOBELLO MUSHROOMS, HALVED

100 GRAMS COURGETTES, SLICED INTO BITE-SIZE PIECES

COCONUT OIL

2 SHALLOTS, SLICED

2 TEASPOONS FENNEL SEEDS

1 FENNEL BULB, STALKS AND LEAVES REMOVED, BULB VERY THINLY SLICED

1 HANDFUL BABY SPINACH, FINELY SLICED

1 SMALL HANDFUL FRESH BASIL LEAVES, FINELY SLICED

±3 TABLESPOONS OLIVE OIL

ZEST AND JUICE OF 1 LEMON

Preheat the oven to 180 °C.

Bring the water and a crack of salt to a boil in a medium-sized saucepan. Rinse the pearl barley and add it to the saucepan. Cook for 30–35 minutes. You don't want it to be too soft, it must still have a slight crunch. Once ready, rinse with cold water, drain and set aside.

Meanwhile, place the mushrooms and courgettes on a roasting tray. Toss with 1 tablespoon coconut oil until evenly coated and season with salt and pepper. Pop the tray into the oven and roast for 35 minutes until golden brown, tossing at the halfway mark. Once ready, remove from the oven.

Meanwhile, in a medium-sized frying pan over medium heat, melt 2 teaspoons coconut oil. Sauté the shallots and fennel seeds for 5–10 minutes until the shallots start to caramelise. Once ready, set aside.

Place the fennel, spinach and basil in a salad bowl and add the pearl barley. Toss until well mixed. Top with the shallots, courgettes and mushrooms. Drizzle over the olive oil and lemon juice and zest. Season to taste and garnish with micro herbs, if desired. Serve right away.

SUMMER SLAW

MANGO, TOMATO AND AVO SALAD

SERVES: 2 | PREPARATION TIME: 20 MINUTES

Combining textures and flavours can result in amazing salads, with this one being a prime example. The mango tastes like summer and its sweet taste is delicious in combination with the acidic tomatoes. The avocado adds a delectable creaminess.

¼ RED ONION, FINELY SLICED

1 TABLESPOON WHITE WINE VINEGAR

2 MEDIUM-SIZED MANGOES, PEELED, PIPS
   REMOVED, CUT INTO CHUNKS

300 GRAMS CHERRY TOMATOES (A VARIETY
   OF COLOURS IF POSSIBLE), SLICED
   AND/OR QUARTERED

1 HANDFUL FRESH CORIANDER LEAVES,
   FINELY SLICED

1 CLOVE GARLIC, MINCED

JUICE OF 1 LIME

1 MEDIUM-SIZED AVOCADO, PEELED, PIP
   REMOVED, CUT INTO CHUNKS

3 TABLESPOONS OLIVE OIL

SALT AND PEPPER

1 HANDFUL WATERCRESS

50 GRAMS RAW ALMONDS, ROUGHLY
   CHOPPED

1 TABLESPOON SUNFLOWER SEEDS

Place the onion slices and vinegar together in a small mixing bowl and set aside for 10 minutes.

Place the mangoes, tomatoes, coriander, garlic, lime juice, avocado and olive oil in a separate mixing bowl. Add the onion slices, season to taste and gently toss everything together.

Transfer to a salad bowl and serve topped with the watercress, almonds and sunflower seeds. Garnish with edible flowers, if desired.

GROUNDED

ROASTED POTATO, PEA AND ASPARAGUS SALAD

SERVES: 4 AS A SIDE | PREPARATION TIME: 10 MINUTES | COOKING TIME: 40 MINUTES

For most of us, staying grounded can be difficult. Life presents so many challenges and this can leave us feeling up in the air. Feelings associated with being ungrounded are anxiety, dizziness, forgetfulness and feeling overwhelmed. One of the ways we can balance out these feelings is by eating root vegetables. This recipe is grounding and just flat out delicious. If you feel you need more grounding in your life, why not try exercising outside, meditation or spending some time in the garden or nature? Observe your feelings when you are in nature. Sunshine and natural surroundings soothe the soul and are a critical part to our wellbeing. Sunshine also creates vitamin D, which protects our immune system amongst other things.

---

500 GRAMS BABY POTATOES, SCRUBBED
COCONUT OIL
1 TEASPOON DRIED OREGANO
SALT AND PEPPER
1 FULL GARLIC BULB, HALVED CROSSWAYS
OLIVE OIL
½ CUP FROZEN OR FRESH PEAS
100 GRAMS FRESH ASPARAGUS, ENDS
   REMOVED, CUT DIAGONALLY INTO
   THIRDS
1 HANDFUL FRESH BASIL LEAVES, FINELY
   CHOPPED
1 SMALL HANDFUL FRESH DILL LEAVES,
   FINELY CHOPPED
1 HANDFUL BABY SPINACH
1 TEASPOON BLACK SESAME SEEDS

DRESSING

ROASTED GARLIC (SEE ABOVE)
½ CUP RAW CASHEW NUTS, SOAKED IN
   WARM WATER FOR AT LEAST 30 MINUTES
⅓ CUP OLIVE OIL
2 TABLESPOONS WHOLEGRAIN DIJON
   MUSTARD
SQUEEZE OF LEMON JUICE (OPTIONAL)
SALT AND PEPPER

Preheat the oven to 180 °C.

Pop the baby potatoes into a medium-sized roasting tin and add 1 tablespoon coconut oil. Toss until evenly covered and season with the oregano and salt and pepper. Add the garlic, keeping the bulb intact, and drizzle with a little melted coconut oil and salt and pepper.

Put the roasting tin into the oven and roast for 30–35 minutes, tossing at the halfway mark. Once golden brown and soft, remove from the oven and pour a good glug of olive oil over the potatoes and garlic. Toss and return to the oven for another 5–10 minutes until they develop a dark golden-brown colour. Once ready, slice in half and set aside to cool.

Meanwhile, fill a medium-sized bowl with just-boiled water and another with ice water. Add the peas and asparagus to the boiled water and blanch for 4 minutes. Remove using a slotted spoon and transfer to the bowl of ice water. Drain and set aside.

For the dressing, squeeze the roasted cloves out of the halved garlic bulb and into a blender. Add the cashew nuts and olive oil and blend until smooth. Add the mustard and lemon juice (if using), season to taste and mix to incorporate.

Place the fresh basil, dill, spinach, asparagus and peas into a large salad bowl. Add the halved potatoes and cover in the dressing. Toss until well combined. Drizzle with extra olive oil and serve with a sprinkling of sesame seeds and a crack of salt and pepper. (Alternatively, plate up with the dressing underneath, as per the photograph.)

WINTER BOWL

ROASTED ROOT VEGETABLE SALAD

SERVES: **4** AS A MAIN, **6** AS A SIDE | PREPARATION TIME: **15** MINUTES | COOKING TIME: **1** HOUR

This dish makes a great main course, but also works as a side dish with meat. I urge you to try the latter first, as this salad has everything you need when it comes to nutrients, comfort and flavour. Meat is always celebrated as the main affair and although I believe in listening to your body when it comes to meat, I also believe in eating plants first and foremost and more often than not. Eating this way is kinder to our planet and to our digestive systems. You will be roasting multiple veggies, so stagger the roasting and prep work in this recipe, especially if your oven is small. If you have a large oven, you can prep all the veggies at once and roast together, saving time.

2 MEDIUM-SIZED SWEET POTATOES,
  SCRUBBED AND CUT INTO
  2 CM THICK DISCS
COCONUT OIL
1 TEASPOON GROUND TURMERIC
SALT AND PEPPER
OLIVE OIL
1 SMALL HEAD CAULIFLOWER, BROKEN
  INTO FLORETS
1 TEASPOON PAPRIKA
250 GRAMS BUTTER BEANS, COOKED (SEE
  PAGE 24)
1 TABLESPOON DUKKAH SPICE
1 TEASPOON YELLOW MUSTARD SEEDS
½ CUP UNCOOKED LENTILS
1 CUP VEGETABLE STOCK
3 LARGE CARROTS, PEELED AND CUT INTO
  2 CM PIECES
3 MEDIUM-SIZED BEETROOTS, WASHED
  AND QUARTERED
1 BUNCH KALE, STALKS REMOVED AND
  LEAVES TORN INTO BITE-SIZE PIECES
1 TEASPOON CAYENNE PEPPER
1 AVOCADO, PEELED, PIP REMOVED, DICED
  (OPTIONAL)
80 GRAMS RAW ALMONDS, ROASTED (SEE
  PAGE 24) AND ROUGHLY CHOPPED

DRESSING

¼ CUP DIJON MUSTARD
¼ CUP HONEY
¼ CUP APPLE CIDER VINEGAR
¼ CUP OLIVE OIL
1 TEASPOON SALT
¼ TEASPOON BLACK PEPPER

Preheat the oven to 180 °C.

Mix together all the ingredients for the dressing and set aside.

Place the sweet potato discs, 1 tablespoon coconut oil and the turmeric into a roasting tin and toss until evenly covered. Season with salt and pepper. Pop into the oven and roast for 45 minutes, tossing the sweet potatoes at the halfway mark. Once ready, remove from the oven, drizzle with olive oil and set aside.

Place the cauliflower florets, paprika and 2 teaspoons coconut oil into a separate roasting tin. Season with salt and pepper and toss until evenly covered. Roast for 30 minutes, tossing 5 minutes before they are ready and making sure to keep an eye on them. You want the edges to be crispy and crunchy. Once the cauliflower is ready, put it in a bowl and set aside.

Place the butter beans and 1 tablespoon coconut oil into the same roasting tin you used for the cauliflower. Add the dukkah spice and mustard seeds and toss until evenly covered. Roast for 30 minutes until crispy, tossing at the halfway mark.

Meanwhile, place the lentils and vegetable stock into a medium-sized saucepan over medium heat and simmer for 35 minutes. You want the lentils to still have a slight crunch. Once ready, drain and set aside.

Place the carrots and beetroots into a roasting dish. Add 2 teaspoons coconut oil and season to taste. Roast for 35 minutes, tossing at the halfway mark. Once golden brown, place the kale leaves on top of the vegetables. Drizzle with olive oil, sprinkle with the cayenne pepper and gently toss until the leaves are evenly covered, but don't mix them with the veg underneath. Roast for an additional 10–15 minutes. Once ready, remove the dish from the oven.

Add the cauliflower and sweet potatoes to the roasting dish with the kale, carrots and beetroots and season to taste.

Add the lentils, butter beans and the dressing and toss well. Transfer to a serving dish and top with the diced avocado (if using) and roasted almonds. Serve warm or at room temperature.

SPRING SHOOTS

GRILLED GREENS

SERVES: 4 | PREPARATION TIME: 10 MINUTES | COOKING TIME: 10 MINUTES

Everyone needs a salad that can be your go-to when hosting a dinner party. This salad is exactly that. It will also inspire you to play around with different greens and you can even add nuts and seeds as a topping. Master this recipe then let your intuition guide you when creating it again. Tuning into your intuition when it comes to food means connecting with the cooking techniques and substituting food of a similar nature. For example, a green bean can be substituted with asparagus or cooked the same way. Have fun and know that salads will never be boring again!

150 GRAMS FRESH ASPARAGUS, ENDS
    REMOVED, HALVED
200 GRAMS TENDER-STEM BROCCOLI,
    HALVED
2 TABLESPOONS OLIVE OIL
SALT AND PEPPER
2 GENEROUS HANDFULS MIXED SALAD
    GREENS OF CHOICE
2 MEDIUM-SIZED COURGETTES, SLICED
    INTO RIBBONS
100 GRAMS SUGAR SNAP PEAS, HALVED
5 RADISHES, THINLY SLICED INTO ROUNDS
1 CUP FROZEN PEAS, BLANCHED
80 GRAMS CHEVIN GOAT'S MILK CHEESE
80 GRAMS RAW WALNUTS, ROASTED (SEE
    PAGE 24)

DRESSING

1 TABLESPOON TAHINI
¼ CUP OLIVE OIL
JUICE OF ½ LEMON
1 TEASPOON HONEY
SALT AND PEPPER

Place the asparagus and broccoli into a large mixing bowl. Add the olive oil, season with salt and pepper and toss until evenly covered.

Bring a griddle pan to a medium to high heat. Add the asparagus and broccoli from the bowl, leaving behind the oil, as you don't want to oil a griddle pan. Grill the vegetables for 4 minutes, covered with a lid, allowing them to steam at the same time as grilling. You can add a tablespoon or two of water to the pan to help them along if need be. Once they have steamed a little, remove the lid and continue grilling for an additional 4 minutes, tossing them often. Once ready, remove from the pan and set aside to cool for 5 minutes.

Mix all the dressing ingredients together, season to taste and set aside.

Place the mixed greens into a large salad dish and get ready to layer your salad. Add the courgette ribbons, sugar snap peas, radishes, peas and grilled greens. Top off with the goat's cheese and walnuts.

Pour over the dressing and gently toss the salad just before serving.

SIDES

This chapter is a homage to vegetables. It shows us that when you take one simple thing and do it to the best of your ability, repeatedly with love, that you can build good eating habits and cooking techniques. The same applies to our lives and how we build healthy habits.

This book and way of being is not about perfection. Perfection doesn't exist. Instead, this journey to health is about a way of being that exists in the beauty that is grey. I know that becoming healthy and staying healthy is hard work, but it is the greatest gift you can give yourself.

Wake up each morning and set yourself one small health goal to achieve that day, and do it repeatedly and well. An example could be to walk for an hour a day or join a Pilates class. Be kind and gentle with yourself. You don't need hours of gym or high-intensity training. You just have to start somewhere small. Before you know it, weeks will go by and fitness will be part of your life and something you crave because of the balance it brings into your life. It all starts with the first little step.

I also want you to think about how the movement of your body connects to your food. Would you put the wrong fuel into your vehicle? No, because it won't run properly if you do. The same applies to your body and food. If you aren't eating well then you won't have the energy to move your body. Your body sees food as one thing and one thing only: fuel (energy). It's your food choices that provide it with good or bad energy. Do you see the cycle? Using mindfulness and willingness we can break a bad cycle and enter a healthier cycle of our lives. You deserve and are worthy of good health.

- How many minutes of cardio do you manage to get in per week?

- How have your parents and grandparents aged, and what aspects of their health do you hope to avoid in your own aging process?

- What parallels can you draw between your current lifestyle choices and theirs that may have a negative or positive impact down the line?

HEALTH TIPS
- A strong cup of chamomile tea can aid sleep as well as work as a very gentle laxative in the morning. Finding a night-time routine and incorporating chamomile tea can be a game changer!
- If you love having fruit as a snack, try adding a handful of raw nuts. The combination of fibre and natural sugar keeps your blood sugar levels stable. The fibre and healthy fats will also help you feel satiated and will stop you from overeating at your next meal.
- When snacking, try to eat fruit earlier in the day and have a high-protein snack at 3 pm to prevent that slump at the end of the day.

GOLDEN POTATOES

TURMERIC AND ROASTED RED PEPPER

SERVES: 6 | PREPARATION TIME: 15 MINUTES | COOKING TIME: 50 MINUTES

Turmeric contains bioactive compounds such as curcumin, which is a very powerful anti-inflammatory, and has been used for centuries as a medicinal plant. Turmeric is very versatile – you can sprinkle it into homemade chocolates, use it in curries or add it to a sponge cake. I sprinkle it over vegetables or add it to rice. Adding black pepper with your curcumin enhances its absorption. Inflammation can be a good thing because it promotes healing, but long-term inflammation can cause chronic disease. To aid digestion and assist with healing gut inflammation, add a ¼ teaspoon turmeric to warm lemon water every morning or buy it in capsule form. Bringing healing spices such as turmeric into your diet not only makes the food flavoursome but also makes it healing.

500 GRAMS BABY POTATOES, SCRUBBED
6 TABLESPOONS OLIVE OIL
3 CLOVES GARLIC, CRUSHED
LEAVES FROM 2 SPRIGS FRESH ROSEMARY
SALT AND PEPPER
2 TEASPOONS COCONUT OIL
1 RED PEPPER, SEEDED AND CUBED
1 TEASPOON GROUND CUMIN
1 TEASPOON GROUND TURMERIC
JUICE OF ½ LEMON
1 HANDFUL FRESH CORIANDER LEAVES,
   ROUGHLY CHOPPED

Preheat the oven to 180 °C.

Pop the potatoes into a saucepan of water – enough to cover them – and boil for 12 minutes until soft when pierced with a fork. Once ready, drain and pop them into a roasting tray. Using the back of a fork, gently press them until they split. Drizzle generously with the olive oil and add the garlic and rosemary in between the potatoes. Season with salt and pepper. Roast for 35 minutes or until the potatoes become golden brown.

Once ready, remove from the oven and cool for 10 minutes.

Meanwhile, heat the coconut oil in a medium-sized frying pan over medium heat. Add the red pepper, cumin and turmeric to the pan and sauté for 2–3 minutes. Add the potatoes to the pan and toss gently. You want them to be crunchy and covered in spice.

To finish off, add the lemon juice and a generous crack of salt. Top with the coriander leaves and serve.

HASSELBACK BUTTERNUT

BLUE CHEESE, WALNUT AND HONEY

SERVES: 4 | PREPARATION TIME: 20 MINUTES | COOKING TIME: 1 HOUR 10 MINUTES

This technique is a really fun one to use on vegetables, especially potatoes, sweet potatoes or even baby potatoes. Every bit of effort that you put into your food and knowing what nourishes you will make it taste even better. It's this connection that's missing in the fast food and take-out world. Love your food and it will love you back. Take time tasting it and adjusting the flavours so that when you eat it you can't contain the love, joy and happiness that you feel.

1 MEDIUM-SIZED BUTTERNUT
1 TABLESPOON COCONUT OIL
3 SPRIGS FRESH ROSEMARY
SALT AND PEPPER
OLIVE OIL
1 TABLESPOON HONEY
80 GRAMS BLUE CHEESE OR
　½ TABLESPOON NUTRITIONAL YEAST
50 GRAMS RAW WALNUTS, ROASTED (SEE
　PAGE 24) AND ROUGHLY CHOPPED

Preheat the oven to 180 °C.

Peel the butternut using a sharp knife or peeler. Once peeled, remove the seeds, halve the butternut lengthways, then slice into the butternut across the width, about halfway through. You need to keep the butternut intact. Slice down the entire length of the butternut, making each slice as thin as possible.

Coat the whole butternut generously with the coconut oil. Place the halves on a roasting tray, flat side down. Tear the rosemary leaves off the sprigs and wedge them between the slices of butternut. Season to taste.

Pop the butternut into the oven and roast for 1 hour, checking at the halfway mark. The longer you roast it (while keeping an eye on it), the yummier it will be. Once the butternut is golden brown and soft with crispy edges, it is ready.

Remove from the oven and drizzle with olive oil and the honey. Pop the butternut back into the oven for 10 minutes.

Once ready, remove the butternut from the oven and crumble over the blue cheese or sprinkle over the nutritional yeast. Add the walnuts and a final crack of salt, and serve with a garnish of herbs of choice.

CRISPY BUTTER BEANS

LEMON, MUSTARD AND BASIL

SERVES: 2 | PREPARATION TIME: 10 MINUTES | COOKING TIME: 20 MINUTES

Beans are so versatile and can be used in stews or curries or a marinated vegetable salad. I do my best to get dried beans, then soak and cook them. It's all part of the process to connect to our food and the journey that it takes to arrive on our plate. We have lost appreciation for where our food comes from, how it was grown or raised and the process it went through to get to us. In turn, if you support healthier processes then you support good health. Healthy eating and living is in every stage of the process and starts with the inception of soil quality. Everything is connected and if we start to make those connections we will start to make healthier choices.

3 TEASPOONS COCONUT OIL

200 GRAMS BUTTER BEANS, COOKED (SEE PAGE 24)

2 TEASPOONS MUSTARD SEEDS

1 LARGE HANDFUL KALE, STALKS REMOVED, AND LEAVES TORN

1 HANDFUL FRESH BASIL LEAVES, FINELY CHOPPED

1 TABLESPOON NUTRITIONAL YEAST

ZEST AND JUICE OF ½ LEMON

OLIVE OIL

SALT AND PEPPER

Heat 2 teaspoons of the coconut oil in a medium-sized frying pan over medium heat. Add the cooked and drained butter beans and cook for 7–10 minutes on one side, giving the pan a gentle shake now and then to make sure they do not stick. If necessary, add a little extra coconut oil.

Once golden brown and crispy on one side, turn the beans over to allow them to cook on the other side. You don't want to turn them too often as they can break apart. Add the mustard seeds at this stage and the remaining teaspoon of coconut oil. You want the seeds to have contact with the pan so they can fry and release their flavour. Add the kale leaves to the butter beans. Gently shake the beans again to ensure they do not stick and cook for an additional 10 minutes.

Remove from the heat and tip into a serving bowl. Add the basil and toss the beans gently until well combined. Add the nutritional yeast, lemon zest and lemon juice. Top with a drizzle of olive oil and a crack of salt and black pepper.

QUICK GREENS

SAUTÉED PAK CHOI AND SHIMEJI MUSHROOMS

SERVES: 2 | PREPARATION TIME: 10 MINUTES | COOKING TIME: 10 MINUTES

This recipe is about simplicity. When I cook, I love to add complexity and big flavours, which often involves a wide variety of ingredients and spices. This recipe, however, is proof that you can create a healthy, tasty dish from a handful of simple ingredients.

2 TEASPOONS COCONUT OIL

200 GRAMS TENDER-STEM BROCCOLI

150 GRAMS SHIMEJI MUSHROOMS

200 GRAMS PAK CHOI

1 TABLESPOON LIQUID AMINOS OR TAMARI

2 TEASPOONS SESAME OIL

2 TEASPOONS BLACK SESAME SEEDS

Heat the coconut oil in a medium-sized frying pan over medium to high heat. Add the tender-stem broccoli and sauté for 3–4 minutes, tossing regularly. Turn the heat up slightly, add the shimeji mushrooms and sauté for an additional 5 minutes. Add the pak choi and toss until the leaves start to wilt, roughly 2 minutes.

Once the mushrooms are cooked and the pak choi has wilted, remove the pan from the heat and stir in the liquid aminos or tamari and the sesame oil. Transfer to a serving bowl and sprinkle with the sesame seeds.

BEETROOT HUMMUS

ROASTED BABY POTATOES AND BRUSSELS SPROUTS

SERVES: 5 | PREPARATION TIME: 20 MINUTES | COOKING TIME: 50 MINUTES

Making healthy eating easy is key. No one wants to spend two hours creating a perfect dish if they are starving and have not eaten the whole day. You also can't expect yourself to make healthier choices in those moments. This recipe ticks all the right boxes as it is easy and can form part of meal prep for the week ahead too.

500 GRAMS BABY POTATOES, SCRUBBED
SALT AND PEPPER
2 TABLESPOONS OLIVE OIL, PLUS EXTRA
1 TEASPOON PAPRIKA
2 TABLESPOONS CHOPPED FRESH
    ROSEMARY LEAVES
200 GRAMS BRUSSELS SPROUTS
2 TABLESPOONS MELTED COCONUT OIL
50 GRAMS SUNFLOWER SEEDS, TOASTED
    (OPTIONAL, SEE PAGE 24)
1 HANDFUL ROCKET
JUICE OF ½ LEMON

HUMMUS

250 GRAMS CHICKPEAS, COOKED (SEE
    PAGE 24)
2 MEDIUM-SIZED BEETROOTS, WASHED,
    QUARTERED AND ROASTED (SEE
    PAGE 76) OR BOILED
2 TABLESPOONS TAHINI
8 TABLESPOONS OLIVE OIL
1 TEASPOON GROUND TURMERIC
½ TEASPOON GROUND CUMIN
1 CLOVE GARLIC
JUICE OF 1 LEMON
SALT AND PEPPER

Preheat the oven to 180 °C.

For the hummus, blend all the ingredients together. Add a little more olive oil if the blender gets stuck. Adjust seasoning if necessary and set aside.

Place the potatoes in a medium-sized saucepan of boiling water with a bit of salt. Boil for 10 minutes or until they are soft when pierced with a fork. Once ready, drain and let them cool on a roasting tray.

Gently squash the potatoes using the back of a fork. Drizzle with the olive oil and sprinkle with the paprika and rosemary. Season with salt and pepper.

Place the Brussels sprouts and melted coconut oil in a bowl. Toss until the sprouts are evenly coated. Season with salt and pepper. Transfer them to the roasting tray with the potatoes.

Pop the veggies into the oven and roast for 40 minutes. Toss the Brussels sprouts at the halfway mark and check on the potatoes. Once golden brown, add a drizzle of olive oil and return to the oven for an additional 10 minutes or until you have golden brown and crunchy potatoes with soft Brussels sprouts. Once ready, remove from the oven.

Spoon the hummus into a serving bowl and drizzle with olive oil. Sprinkle half the sunflower seeds (if using) over the dip and top with rocket or baby beetroot leaves. Arrange the potatoes and Brussels sprouts on a serving platter and sprinkle with the remaining sunflower seeds (if using) and a lashing of lemon juice. Serve with the hummus on the side.

SWEET RED RICE

ALMONDS, ORANGE AND DATES

SERVES: 4 | PREPARATION TIME: 10 MINUTES | COOKING TIME: 40 MINUTES

Time is such a special thing. We can't get it back and when we do look at the past it can overwhelm us with a sense of nostalgia. The people we share laughter with and who feed our souls are part of our good health. Nurture those relationships with healthy boundaries and bring love into your life. Good health also means letting go of grudges and healing past wounds. Do your best to make the most of the time you have and spend it wisely.

1½ TEASPOONS SAFFRON THREADS

1 CUP UNCOOKED RED RICE

PINCH OF SALT

5 TABLESPOONS GHEE OR BUTTER

90 GRAMS RAW ALMONDS, ROASTED (SEE PAGE 24) AND CHOPPED

6 MEDJOOL DATES, PITTED AND CHOPPED

½ TEASPOON WHITE PEPPER

1 TEASPOON GROUND TURMERIC

½ TABLESPOON ORANGE ZEST

Place the saffron in a small glass with 3 tablespoons warm water. Set aside.

Place the rice and 2 cups water into a medium-sized saucepan. Add the salt and cook for 20–25 minutes or until done. Once the rice is ready and the water has cooked off, remove from the heat and set aside. Keep the lid on so that the rice steams.

Place 4 tablespoons of the ghee with the almonds and dates into a separate saucepan over medium heat. Add the white pepper and turmeric and fry for 5 minutes, stirring often.

Spoon the red rice over the almond mixture and mix until combined. Add 3 tablespoons boiling water then add in the final tablespoon of ghee and a crack of salt and the saffron with water. Cover with a lid and cook over low to medium heat for 10 minutes, then turn the heat off and keep the lid on. Allow the top part of the rice to steam and the bottom to fry. Make sure it doesn't burn, but don't stir the rice.

Place a serving plate over the top of the saucepan and gently flip the rice out. Sprinkle over the orange zest, garnish with micro herbs, if desired, and serve hot.

ROASTED SWEET POTATO

WITH PARSLEY AND WALNUT PESTO

SERVES: 4 | PREPARATION TIME: 10 MINUTES | COOKING TIME: 1 HOUR 10 MINUTES

What sets your soul on fire when it comes to creativity? Is this something you have explored? Tuning into your inner child offers you the chance to play. Playfulness leads to experimentation and if you do so without judgement you will be surprised at what you can create, not only in the kitchen but also in your life. Expressing yourself creatively offers you a chance to de-stress and connect with yourself.

1 KG SWEET POTATOES, SCRUBBED AND
    CUT INTO THICK WEDGES
2 TABLESPOONS COCONUT OIL
SALT AND PEPPER
OLIVE OIL
MALDON SALT

PARSLEY AND WALNUT PESTO

1 BUNCH FRESH FLAT-LEAF PARSLEY
JUICE AND ZEST OF 1 LEMON
90 GRAMS RAW WALNUTS
1 CLOVE GARLIC
6 TABLESPOONS OLIVE OIL
SALT AND PEPPER

Preheat the oven to 180 °C. Line a large roasting tray with baking paper.

Place the sweet potato wedges and coconut oil into a large bowl. Toss until the wedges are evenly coated in oil. Place the wedges, skin-side down, on the prepared tray and season with salt and pepper. Pop them into the oven and roast for 1 hour and 10 minutes, turning them at the 45-minute mark. Ten to fifteen minutes before they are ready, drizzle them with some olive oil and allow them to finish roasting.

While the wedges are roasting, place the parsley, lemon juice, walnuts, garlic and olive oil into a blender. Blend until you reach a smooth, creamy consistency. Season to taste and fold through the lemon zest.

Once the sweet potatoes are golden brown (I like my edges crunchy), remove them from the oven. Add a few dollops of the pesto to the wedges and toss them gently until evenly coated.

Transfer the wedges to a serving bowl and sprinkle with Maldon salt and some ground black pepper. Garnish with micro herbs, if desired, and serve hot.

OLIVE GROVE

SOURDOUGH FLATBREAD WITH TAPENADE

SERVES: **4** | PREPARATION TIME: **15** MINUTES | COOKING TIME: **20** MINUTES

Cooking with intuition is half the fun in the kitchen. If you take the time to tap into what your body is craving, you can choose to nourish it with wholesome food that will satisfy you. For this recipe you can either make olive tapenade yourself or marinate some vegetables. If you choose to buy store-bought products, make sure that you read the ingredients label so that you buy the healthiest choice. In the case of tapenade, it should ideally only include olives, capers, some olive oil and salt. Olives are high in vitamin E and filled with powerful antioxidants. For this recipe, you only need a quarter portion of the sourdough. I prepare a full portion, use roughly a quarter for this recipe and then simply use the rest of the dough to bake a smaller loaf for the next day.

SOURDOUGH FLATBREAD

¼ PORTION SOURDOUGH (SEE PAGE 42)

2 TABLESPOONS ROUGHLY CHOPPED
FRESH ROSEMARY LEAVES

1 CLOVE GARLIC, FINELY CHOPPED

2 TEASPOONS SALT

1 TABLESPOON OLIVE OIL

TAPENADE

250 GRAMS OLIVES, PITTED

2 TABLESPOONS FRESH CAPERS

½ TEASPOON CHOPPED FRESH CHILLI

JUICE OF ½ LEMON

BLACK PEPPER TO TASTE

5 TABLESPOONS OLIVE OIL

For the tapenade, place all the ingredients, except the olive oil, into a food processor and blend until roughly chopped. Add the olive oil and continue blending until a chunky paste forms. Serve immediately in a bowl with the warm flatbread or spoon into a sterilised glass jar and cover with a thin layer of olive oil. It will keep in the fridge for up to a week.

To make the flatbread, preheat the oven to 180 °C. Lightly oil a baking tray.

Using your hands, stretch out the dough into the shape of a flatbread, roughly 15 x 25 cm. It's okay if it isn't perfectly shaped, nothing in life really is. You want it to be roughly 1 cm thick. Place the dough onto the prepared tray and sprinkle the rosemary, garlic and salt over the sourdough. Pop the tray into the oven for 20 minutes or until the flatbread is golden brown. Once ready, brush lightly with the olive oil and serve warm.

THE PERFECT MASH

SWEET POTATO AND ROASTED LEMON

SERVES: 4 AS A SIDE | PREPARATION TIME: 15 MINUTES | COOKING TIME: 45–60 MINUTES

There are so many conflicting opinions on how we should nourish ourselves – it can become overwhelming at times. I want you to tune into your inner voice, the one that knows the answer to your questions. It's the voice that tells us to slow down and pay attention to the messages our bodies are sending us about which foods are best for us at any given moment. These messages can be transmitted in a variety of ways, such as genuine hunger, cravings, addictions, allergies, good and bad moods, energy levels from high to low, physical discomfort, and pleasurable sensations. As you begin to understand the subtleties of your personal nutrition, you will also understand what all of these signals mean and which dish will nourish your body in tune with your inner voice.

2 KG SWEET POTATOES, HALF PEELED AND
  HALF UNPEELED
3 TABLESPOONS COCONUT OIL
3 LEMONS
1 FULL GARLIC BULB, HALVED CROSSWAYS
OLIVE OIL
2 TABLESPOONS COCONUT SUGAR
2 TABLESPOONS RED WINE VINEGAR
JUICE OF 1 ORANGE
1–2 RED CHILLIES, CHOPPED
3 TABLESPOONS CHOPPED FRESH
  SAGE LEAVES
1 TABLESPOON FRESH THYME LEAVES
SALT AND PEPPER

Preheat the oven to 180 °C.

Toss the whole sweet potatoes with 2 tablespoons of the coconut oil in a large bowl. Once coated, pop them onto a roasting tray and roast for 45 minutes until they are soft when pierced with a fork. Once ready, set aside to cool.

Slice the lemons about 1 cm thick and remove all the seeds. Add the slices to a small bowl and toss with the remaining 1 tablespoon coconut oil. Place the lemons and garlic onto a separate roasting tray, drizzle a little olive oil on the garlic, and roast for 25 minutes or until the lemon slices are soft and golden. Once ready, set aside.

Place the coconut sugar, red wine vinegar and orange juice into a medium-sized saucepan over medium heat. Add the chillies and cook for 15 minutes, reducing the mixture. You want it to become darker in colour and syrupy.

Place the cooled sweet potatoes into a large bowl and mash them to a chunky consistency. Add the reduced sauce and herbs and mash together.

Squeeze the roasted gloves out of the halved garlic bulb casing and roughly chop together with the lemons. Add the lemon and garlic to the sweet potatoes and mix until combined. Season to taste with salt and pepper.

Garnish with fresh thyme leaves and serve hot or at room temperature.

BROTHS AND SOUPS

Broths and soups are incredibly healing because they are a melting pot of spices, herbs and vegetables. Often, when we steam or boil food, nutrients can be lost to the water, but with soups all the vitamins, minerals and health properties stay in one pot, especially if you combine a variety of vegetables. They are also mineral rich and easy to digest.

The more vegetables you add, the more healing properties you can benefit from. For example: carrots help lower blood pressure and balance cognitive function, onions and garlic have antiviral and antibacterial properties and can eliminate heavy toxins and metals from the body, parsley and shiitake mushrooms are an incredible source of iron and zinc, the latter supporting our immune system and skin health, and ginger and turmeric are healing for the liver and are powerful anti-inflammatories.

When you are sick or feeling run down, I suggest tucking into this chapter. It will keep you warm in winter and support your body with a maximum intake of nutrients. The soups and broths keep well in the fridge and often the flavours develop even more overnight. If you are meal prepping, then you can also freeze a batch of soup and save it for later on. Just remember to add a handful of fresh greens, such as baby spinach, when reheating.

- How can you start to become more accountable to yourself in your relationship with food?

- What excuses do you make when it comes to your food choices?

- What health concerns do you have and how long have you had them?

HEALTH TIPS
- Juicing can be very beneficial for health. When it comes to juicing, the greener the better. Try to focus on vegetable juice rather than too much fruit juice, as fruit juice can become a strong sugar hit for your blood sugar levels once the fibre has been removed. Green juice with spinach, lemon, celery and kale can be a great nutrient hit for your liver.
- Detox your environment. Check how many of your products that you use on your body and in your home are filled with harmful chemicals. Slowly but surely replace a finished product with a better alternative that is not only healthier for you but also environmentally friendly.
- Rushing and stressing can cause your cortisol levels to go through the roof, which leads to your body naturally holding onto weight. Part of managing your stress is not only about time management but also being internally kinder to yourself. Have you taken three deep breaths today? What can you do better to manage your time? Try leaving little messages of love for yourself everywhere – in your diary, on your mirror or on the fridge door.

HEARTY WHOLE SOUP

COCONUT AND RED LENTIL SOUP WITH CASHEW CREAM

SERVES: 4 | PREPARATION TIME: 15 MINUTES | COOKING TIME: 1 HOUR

Red lentils are a wonderful addition to any soup because they're high in protein and they cook relatively quickly. They bulk up a soup and create a hearty, warming dish with minimal effort. The cashew cream is delicious and adds a richness to the dish that will leave you wanting more. Cashew nuts are rich in selenium, zinc, magnesium, iron and phosphorus. Also, they are great sources of phytochemicals, proteins and antioxidants. The high percentage of selenium in cashew nuts means they are wondrously good for your skin. This means glowing skin and delicious food.

CASHEW CREAM

- ½ CUP RAW CASHEW NUTS, SOAKED OVERNIGHT OR FOR AT LEAST 4 HOURS IN WARM WATER
- 1 TABLESPOON FRESHLY SQUEEZED LIME JUICE
- 1 CUP FRESH CORIANDER LEAVES
- ½ CUP WATER
- 1 TABLESPOON HONEY
- SALT TO TASTE

COCONUT AND RED LENTIL SOUP

- 1 RED ONION, DICED
- 2 TEASPOONS COCONUT OIL
- 2 CLOVES GARLIC, MINCED
- 1 TEASPOON GROUND TURMERIC
- ½ TEASPOON CAYENNE PEPPER
- 1 TEASPOON SMOKED PAPRIKA
- 1 TEASPOON GROUND CORIANDER
- 6 PLUM TOMATOES, DICED
- 1 MEDIUM-SIZED CARROT, SCRUBBED AND GRATED
- 1 SMALL SWEET POTATO, SCRUBBED AND CUBED
- 3 CUPS VEGETABLE STOCK
- 1 CUP COCONUT MILK
- 1 CUP WATER
- ½ CUP UNCOOKED RED SPLIT LENTILS
- ½ CUP UNCOOKED WILD BROWN RICE
- ½ BUNCH KALE, STALKS REMOVED AND LEAVES TORN
- 1 HANDFUL FRESH BASIL LEAVES, FINELY CHOPPED
- SALT AND PEPPER
- OLIVE OIL
- 1 LEMON

For the cashew cream, place all the ingredients into a high-speed blender and blend until smooth. You can store what you don't use in an airtight container in the fridge for up to 3 days.

For the soup, place the onion and coconut oil in a medium-sized saucepan over medium heat. Sauté for 10 minutes. Add the garlic, turmeric, cayenne pepper, paprika and coriander and sauté for a further 5 minutes. Add the tomatoes, carrot and sweet potato and cook for 5 minutes, stirring often.

Add the stock, coconut milk and water along with the red lentils and brown rice. Simmer with the lid on for 40 minutes. If the water level gets too low, you can top it up a bit. Once the rice has cooked through, the soup is ready. Remove from the heat and stir in the kale and basil. Season to taste with salt and pepper.

Serve with a generous drizzle of olive oil and add a dollop of the cashew cream and a squeeze of lemon.

SWEET CHOWDER

CORN AND CASHEW

SERVES: 4 | PREPARATION TIME: 15 MINUTES | COOKING TIME: 40 MINUTES

This is my take on a classic. Inspired by clam chowder, this recipe is the plant-based version that packs in all the flavour and has the perfect contrast between sweet and sour. The warming spices are also incredibly healing for the digestive system, so I encourage you to play around with the heat in this soup. Spices such as cayenne pepper can help fire up the digestive system, which supports the assimilation of nutrients into the body.

1 TABLESPOON COCONUT OIL

1 BROWN ONION, DICED

2 CLOVES GARLIC, DICED

2 TEASPOONS GROUND TURMERIC

¼ TEASPOON CAYENNE PEPPER

2 TEASPOONS GROUND CUMIN

5 COBS SWEETCORN

1 YELLOW PEPPER, SEEDED AND CHOPPED

4 CUPS VEGETABLE STOCK

½ CUP COCONUT MILK

½ CUP RAW CASHEW NUTS, SOAKED
   OVERNIGHT OR FOR AT LEAST 4 HOURS
   IN WARM WATER

SALT AND PEPPER

1 HANDFUL FRESH CORIANDER LEAVES

2 LIMES

Heat the coconut oil in a medium-sized saucepan over medium heat. Add the onion and sauté for 5 minutes until translucent. Add the garlic and spices and sauté for a further 5 minutes. If necessary, add a splash of water to help it along.

Remove the kernels from the sweetcorn by cutting down the length of the cobs. Add the corn kernels and the yellow pepper to the saucepan along with the vegetable stock and coconut milk. Simmer for 20 minutes to develop the flavours.

Once cooked, remove half the soup and blend it together with the soaked cashew nuts using either a stick or high-speed blender. (You can blend all of it, but I like it with some whole kernels mixed in.) Return the blended soup to the saucepan and mix together. Let it simmer for an additional 10 minutes.

Season to taste with salt and pepper and serve with some fresh coriander on top and a squeeze of lime.

SALT AND SMOKE

SWEET POTATO AND CAULIFLOWER SOUP

SERVES: 4 | PREPARATION TIME: 15 MINUTES | COOKING TIME: 1 HOUR

Eating salt in real food with balance can supply the body with vital minerals. Eating salty foods that are processed or overly salty can send us down the rabbit hole of cravings. Do you see the feedback loop? When you balance your food in flavour and focus on real foods the taste buds and body feel satisfied and cravings can settle. My first advice when you have a craving is always to first have a glass of water. This can stabilise the body's homeostasis and create space between us and a massive craving. Capers and almonds create a beautiful combination with the earthiness of the sweet potato and the cauliflower in this soup. Focusing on contrasting flavours is what helps us reach the umami moment with our food.

1 MEDIUM-SIZED HEAD CAULIFLOWER,
   BROKEN INTO FLORETS
COCONUT OIL
1 TEASPOON SMOKED PAPRIKA
1 BROWN ONION, CHOPPED
1 CLOVE GARLIC, MINCED
2 TEASPOONS GROUND CUMIN
3 PURPLE (OR WHITE OR YELLOW) SWEET
   POTATOES, SCRUBBED AND CUBED
4 CUPS VEGETABLE STOCK
SALT AND PEPPER
1 TABLESPOON CAPER BERRIES
40 GRAMS RAW ALMONDS,
   ROUGHLY CHOPPED
OLIVE OIL

Preheat the oven to 180 °C.

In a small bowl, toss half the cauliflower with 1 tablespoon coconut oil and the smoked paprika. Pop the cauliflower onto a roasting tray and roast for 30 minutes, tossing at the halfway mark. You want the edges to become crispy. Once ready, set aside.

While the cauliflower is roasting, heat 1 tablespoon coconut oil in a medium-sized saucepan over medium heat. Add the onion and sauté for 5 minutes until translucent. Add the garlic and sauté for a further 3 minutes. Add the cumin and sauté for 2 minutes to release the flavours, then add the sweet potatoes and the uncooked half of the cauliflower florets. Cover the vegetables in the stock and bring to a simmer for 30 minutes until the vegetables are cooked and soft. Once ready, blend the soup using a stick or high-speed blender and season to taste.

Heat 1 teaspoon coconut oil in a small frying pan and fry the caper berries for 4 minutes. Add the almonds and toast together for another minute.

Serve the soup hot, topped with the crunchy cauliflower florets, crispy capers and almonds. Finish it off with a drizzle of olive oil and a crack of black pepper.

HEALING BROTH

TURMERIC AND GINGER

SERVES: 4 | PREPARATION TIME: 20 MINUTES | COOKING TIME: 1 HOUR

Taking time to explore somewhere new can feed the soul and teach us about new cultures and give us profound perspective into our own lives. You don't have to go far, but you do need to disconnect. Good health is not only in the tactile form but also in the energetic space of experiences, laughter, sharing an ice cream with a loved one or exploring a new city by foot. This soup is light and easy on the digestive system. The turmeric is a powerful anti-inflammatory and the range of raw toppings makes it light and energising. I encourage you to play around with different toppings and use this base as inspiration to get creative.

BROTH

- 4 CUPS VEGETABLE STOCK
- 2 LARGE LEEKS, SLICED
- 1 BROWN ONION, SLICED
- 2 CLOVES GARLIC, MINCED
- 2 FRESH RED CHILLIES, ROUGHLY CHOPPED
- 2 LARGE CARROTS, SCRUBBED AND ROUGHLY CHOPPED
- 1 CUP SHIITAKE MUSHROOMS, ROUGHLY CHOPPED
- ½ HEAD GREEN CABBAGE, ROUGHLY CHOPPED
- 4 STALKS CELERY, ROUGHLY CHOPPED
- 2 THUMB-SIZE PIECE FRESH GINGER, PEELED
- 2 TABLESPOONS FRESHLY GRATED TURMERIC OR 1 TABLESPOON GROUND TURMERIC
- 2 HANDFULS FRESH FLAT-LEAF PARSLEY LEAVES
- SALT AND PEPPER
- OLIVE OIL
- 2 LIMES

SUGGESTED TOPPINGS

- ¼ BUNCH KALE, STALKS REMOVED AND LEAVES FINELY SLICED
- 1 SMALL HANDFUL FRESH MIXED SPROUTS
- ¼ CUP SHREDDED RED CABBAGE
- 20 GRAMS FRESH BASIL LEAVES, FINELY SLICED
- 100 GRAMS BROCCOLI, BLANCHED
- 1 SHALLOT, FINELY SLICED
- CRUNCHY CHICKPEAS (SEE PAGE 149)
- 1 CUP COOKED BROWN RICE

For the broth, pour the stock plus 2 cups water into a large saucepan over medium heat and bring to a boil.

Add all the vegetables, ginger, turmeric and parsley leaves to the saucepan and simmer for 1 hour. If you're really pushed for time, 45 minutes will do but you really want to cook it for longer if possible. If the liquid gets too low, top it up with hot water.

Once ready, strain the broth, keeping the liquid and discarding the vegetables. You can save your vegetables and add them to a compost heap or feed them to your chickens if you have. Season the broth with salt and pepper.

While the broth is simmering, prepare the toppings. You can serve the kale, sprouts, cabbage and basil raw, but you'll need to cook the broccoli and shallot.

Heat 1 teaspoon coconut oil in a small frying pan over medium heat and lightly sauté the broccoli for 5 minutes. Set aside.

Heat ½ cup sunflower oil in a small saucepan over medium heat. Once the oil is hot, add the shallot and deep-fry for 8–10 minutes until crispy. Once ready, remove from the oil using a slotted spoon and pop onto some paper towel to remove the excess oil.

Once your broth is ready, set out all the toppings in separate bowls and combine as you wish. Serve with a drizzle of olive oil and a squeeze of fresh lime.

TOMATO AND PEA

LENTIL SOUP WITH GARLIC BREAD

SERVES: 4 | PREPARATION TIME: 15 MINUTES | COOKING TIME: 1 HOUR 15 MINUTES

I want you to learn to fail yourself to success. Both in the kitchen and in your life. Our lives are not defined by all the moments that go right. It is defined by the moments where things go wrong and we course correct with courage. You don't always have to get it right. There will be times where you overeat, there will be times that you make the less healthier food choice. It's okay. Learn to let it go and to be kind to yourself. Soup is an incredible way to pack in all the nutrients your body needs. This soup is full of protein in the lentils and fibre in the vegetables which is good for your gut health as well as keeping you fuller for longer.

BREAD DOUGH

- 1½ CUPS BROWN RICE FLOUR
- 1¼ CUPS WHITE RICE FLOUR
- 3 TABLESPOONS TAPIOCA FLOUR
- 2 TEASPOONS SALT
- 3 HEAPED TEASPOONS BAKING POWDER
- ¼ TEASPOON BICARBONATE OF SODA
- 1 TABLESPOON APPLE CIDER VINEGAR
- 1½ CUPS WATER
- 50 GRAMS RAW WALNUTS, FINELY CHOPPED
- 1 TABLESPOON PUMPKIN SEEDS
- 1 TABLESPOON SUNFLOWER SEEDS

GARLIC MIXTURE

- 1 TABLESPOON FINELY CHOPPED FRESH
  ROSEMARY LEAVES
- 3 CLOVES GARLIC, FINELY MINCED
- OLIVE OIL

SOUP

- 1 TABLESPOON COCONUT OIL
- 1 BROWN ONION, FINELY CHOPPED
- 2 CLOVES GARLIC, FINELY SLICED
- 1 TABLESPOON FRESH THYME LEAVES
- 4 BAY LEAVES
- 1 TEASPOON DRIED OREGANO
- 1 TEASPOON DRIED RED CHILLI FLAKES
- 6 PLUM TOMATOES, FINELY CHOPPED
- 1 LARGE LEEK, FINELY SLICED
- 1 LARGE CARROT, SCRUBBED AND GRATED
- 1 CUP UNCOOKED BROWN LENTILS
- 4 CUPS VEGETABLE STOCK
- ½ CUP FRESH OR FROZEN PEAS
- 1 HANDFUL FLAT-LEAF PARSLEY LEAVES
- SALT AND PEPPER
- ¼ CUP COCONUT CREAM

Preheat the oven to 180 °C. Line a bread tin with baking paper. This will make sure your bread stays intact and makes it easier to lift out once it's ready.

For the bread dough, place all the ingredients, except the pumpkin and sunflower seeds, into a large bowl. Mix until well combined and the batter is smooth. Tip the mixture into the prepared bread tin and sprinkle over the pumpkin and sunflower seeds. Fill a separate baking dish with boiling water. Place the bread tin into the water bath, pop into the oven and bake for 45 minutes. The water will help steam the bread while it bakes.

Meanwhile, make the soup. Heat the coconut oil in a medium-sized saucepan over medium heat. Add the onion and sauté for 5 minutes until translucent. Add the garlic, thyme, bay leaves, oregano and chilli flakes. Mix well and sauté for 5 minutes. Add the tomatoes and stir well, cooking them for 10 minutes to reduce the acidity.

Add the leek and carrot and cook for 10 minutes. If the mixture starts to stick, add a little water to help it along. Once the mixture has cooked, add the lentils and vegetable stock. Bring to a boil over high heat, then reduce to a simmer. Cook for 45 minutes, stirring every 10 minutes. If the liquid gets too low, top it up with boiling water. You want a thick soup consistency. Once the soup is ready, remove from the heat and stir in the peas and parsley. Season to taste.

Once the bread is ready, remove from the oven and turn the oven down to 160 °C. Place the rosemary and garlic into a small bowl and stir together until well mixed.

Once the bread has cooled enough to handle it, slice as much as you like and place the slices on a baking tray. Drizzle olive oil (roughly 1 or 2 tablespoons) onto the bread slices and cover with the garlic mixture. Bake for 10 minutes until lightly toasted.

Once everything is ready, serve the soup with a lick of coconut cream on top and the garlic bread on the side. Only thing left to do is decide whether you're a dunker or a dipper!

SPICED

ROASTED CARROT AND CARDAMOM SOUP

SERVES: 2 | PREPARATION TIME: 15 MINUTES | COOKING TIME: 1 HOUR

Roasting the carrots before adding them enhances the richness of this soup. This is again an example of how time and heat in the kitchen are powerful tools for creating magnificent depth of flavour. The longer you cook something, the more the flavours are going to develop. Carrots are a great source of betacarotene, fibre and vitamin K, which means they support eye health and lower cholesterol.

600 GRAMS CARROTS, SCRUBBED
  AND CHOPPED
COCONUT OIL
4–5 CARDAMOM PODS
SALT AND PEPPER
2 SHALLOTS, FINELY SLICED
2 CLOVES GARLIC, FINELY SLICED
1 TABLESPOON GRATED FRESH GINGER
½ TEASPOON GROUND CUMIN
½ TEASPOON GROUND CORIANDER
½ TEASPOON GROUND TURMERIC
½ TEASPOON CAYENNE PEPPER
3 CUPS VEGETABLE STOCK
1 CUP COCONUT MILK
OLIVE OIL

Preheat the oven to 180 °C.

Place the carrots, 1 tablespoon coconut oil and the cardamom pods into a roasting tin and toss until the carrots are evenly coated in oil. Season with salt and pepper and pop them into the oven for 30 minutes until they are soft and roasted.

Meanwhile, heat 2 teaspoons coconut oil in a large saucepan over medium heat. Add the shallots and sauté for roughly 5 minutes until translucent. Add the garlic and sauté for a further 5 minutes, stirring often. Add the ginger and spices and sauté until aromatic. Add the roasted carrots, vegetable stock and coconut milk and bring to a simmer. Simmer for 30 minutes.

Remove from the heat and blend using a stick or high-speed blender until smooth. Season to taste with salt and pepper and serve with a drizzle of olive oil or some extra coconut milk.

BUTTER BEAN BROTH

WITH KALE AND TOMATOES

SERVES: 2 | PREPARATION TIME: 15 MINUTES | COOKING TIME: 45 MINUTES

Butter beans are one of my favourite beans to cook with. They're an excellent source of dietary fibre, protein and B vitamins, which makes them a happy food. They can also help reduce blood sugar and improve cholesterol levels. You can roast them, sauté them or add them to a soup. Any way you choose, they're bound to make a delicious meal.

1 TABLESPOON COCONUT OIL

1 BROWN ONION, FINELY SLICED

2 CLOVES GARLIC, MINCED

1 LARGE CARROT, SCRUBBED AND
    FINELY SLICED

2 STALKS CELERY, FINELY SLICED

5 PLUM TOMATOES, FINELY DICED

3 TABLESPOONS TOMATO PASTE

2 TEASPOONS DRIED OREGANO

3 BAY LEAVES

6 BABY POTATOES, SCRUBBED AND HALVED

4 CUPS VEGETABLE STOCK

1 CUP BUTTER BEANS, COOKED (SEE
    PAGE 24)

1 BUNCH KALE, STALKS REMOVED AND
    LEAVES TORN

¼ CUP NUTRITIONAL YEAST OR GRATED
    PARMESAN CHEESE

SALT AND PEPPER

OLIVE OIL

JUICE OF ½ LEMON

Heat the coconut oil in a medium-sized saucepan over medium heat. Add the onion and garlic and sauté for 5 minutes. Add the carrot and celery and cook for an additional 5 minutes until the vegetables have softened. Add the tomatoes and tomato paste, stirring well. Add the oregano and bay leaves along with the potatoes. Pour in the stock and let it simmer for 25 minutes.

Add the butter beans and cook for 10 minutes. Add the kale and nutritional yeast or Parmesan and stir well. Season to taste.

Serve hot with a drizzle of olive oil, lemon juice and a crack of black pepper.

REFRESH

COOLING CUCUMBER SOUP

SERVES: 6 | PREPARATION TIME: 10 MINUTES

This is a very cooling soup for the digestive system. If you find you are having an emotional or physical Pitta dosha reaction (as with Ayurveda, see page 9), such as heartburn, then this is the soup for you. It can also aid in more subliminal reactions in your life. Next time you find yourself in a reactive state, try to ground yourself through breathing as well as cooling foods such as this soup. Another benefit is that the cucumbers help keep you hydrated and can support stress management because they are very high in multiple B vitamins. This soup is best served fresh on a summer's day!

3 AVOCADOS, PEELED AND PIP REMOVED
¼ CUP WATER
1 HANDFUL BABY SPINACH
4 CUCUMBERS, PEELED AND CUT
   INTO CHUNKS
1 TABLESPOON CHOPPED FRESH
   DILL LEAVES
1 SHALLOT, FINELY CHOPPED
2 TABLESPOONS APPLE CIDER VINEGAR
SALT AND PEPPER TO TASTE
¼ CUP OLIVE OIL, PLUS EXTRA

Place all the ingredients into a blender and blend until smooth and creamy. Dress with a generous drizzle of olive oil and some black pepper and a garnish of choice, such as edible flowers, toasted pumpkin seeds, extra chopped cucumber and micro herbs. Serve immediately.

MISO BROTH

WALNUT AND CRISPY TOFU

SERVES: 4 | PREPARATION TIME: 15 MINUTES | COOKING TIME: 20 MINUTES

Time is the one thing we never seem to have enough of and our first excuse when it comes to why we aren't achieving our goals. This recipe is quick and easy to make, and incredibly good for your gut microbiome. Miso is a fermented food, which means it is great for gut health and adds a beautiful depth of flavour to a quick and easy broth. Having good gut health not only ensures that you don't have an array of digestive issues, but can also assist you with mental health issues. Healing your gut means happier moods. Time management aids you in combating stress and supports healthy habits.

1 TABLESPOON COCONUT OIL
250 GRAMS TOFU, CUBED

BROTH

4 CUPS VEGETABLE STOCK
2 SHEETS NORI, FINELY SLICED
1 BUNCH SWISS CHARD, STALKS REMOVED
    AND LEAVES ROUGHLY CHOPPED
¼ CUP FINELY SLICED SPRING ONION
1 THUMB-SIZE PIECE FRESH GINGER,
    PEELED AND CUT INTO MATCHSTICKS
1 CUP SHIMEJI MUSHROOMS
250 GRAMS PAK CHOI
SESAME OIL
250 GRAMS BUCKWHEAT NOODLES
OLIVE OIL
1 TEASPOON LIQUID AMINOS

MISO PASTE

120 GRAMS RAW WALNUTS, ROASTED (SEE
    PAGE 24)
¼ CUP BROWN RICE MISO PASTE
1 TABLESPOON HONEY
1 TABLESPOON TAMARI OR SOY SAUCE
2 TEASPOONS WHITE WINE VINEGAR

For the tofu, heat the coconut oil in a medium-sized frying pan over medium heat. Add the tofu cubes and fry for 5 minutes on each side until golden brown. Once ready, remove from the heat, drain on paper towel and set aside.

Now let's get the broth started. Place the vegetable stock, nori, Swiss chard, spring onion and ginger into a medium-sized saucepan over medium heat and bring to a boil. Reduce the heat and simmer for 15 minutes, then switch off the heat. Add the mushrooms and pak choi and stir through. Keep the lid on to retain the heat.

Meanwhile, cook the noodles as per the packet instructions. Once ready, drizzle with olive oil to stop them from sticking together and then set aside.

For the miso paste, place the walnuts into a food processor and blend. Add the remaining ingredients and stir to combine.

Serve the broth with the noodles, crispy tofu and a big dollop of miso paste stirred in. Drizzle over some sesame oil and the liquid aminos for that extra salty kick.

FEASTS

This is the chapter where I truly celebrate the way I love to cook. The recipes take a little longer and the portions are a little larger. Why? Because I believe that sharing food that you made with love around a table with people you love can only bring joy.

Laughter, sleep and a good cup of tea can solve most problems in life. If not, then try cooking one of these meals. Take your time, indulge in the flavours. Pay attention to the way you wash, cut and cook your food. Taste, season and love your food, because if you do, it is going to love you back. Food is the fundamental ingredient, but love is the ultimate flavour.

"Love doesn't need reason. It speaks from the irrational wisdom of the heart." – Deepak Chopra

- What matters most to you in your professional life? What are you most passionate about?

- What skills, talents or competencies do you have that you are most proud of? Which of these makes you the happiest? Which of these makes you feel accomplished?

- What skill or accomplishment would you love to be able to list on your ideal resumé?

HEALTH TIPS

- Make peace with food. It isn't the enemy, nor is your body. Give yourself permission to eat real healthy food and to eat with joy and celebration. Focus on mindful eating, now and always. Three deep breaths before you eat and chew, chew, chew!
- What you hold onto emotionally you will hold onto physically. Be aware of where you are at with kindness and less judgement. Learning to sit with difficult emotions is part of our journey. Food will never solve how you are feeling, but processing your emotions on a healthy level will support you in having a healthier relationship with food.
- Do something nice for someone else today. So often we get caught up in what is going on for us that we forget about what is going on for others. Doing something nice for someone can help your self-esteem and give you a good dose of perspective.

ROASTED MUSHROOM PASTA

CHICKPEAS, LEMON AND RICOTTA

SERVES: 4 | PREPARATION TIME: 10 MINUTES | COOKING TIME: 40 MINUTES

Pasta can be such a tricky ingredient as many people fear carbohydrates as a food group. The reality is that it isn't unhealthy for you unless you are eating it way too often, such as every day. Visit your local health store for healthier pasta alternatives, such as chickpea pasta or buckwheat pasta, which are just as delicious and far more nutritious than regular wheat pastas.

5 LARGE BROWN MUSHROOMS

6 TABLESPOONS MELTED COCONUT OIL

2 TEASPOONS DRIED OREGANO

SALT AND PEPPER

250 GRAMS CHICKPEAS, COOKED (SEE PAGE 24) AND DRAINED

2 CLOVES GARLIC

1 TABLESPOON CHOPPED FRESH ROSEMARY LEAVES

250 GRAMS BUCKWHEAT PENNE OR OTHER PASTA OF YOUR CHOICE

2–3 TABLESPOONS OLIVE OIL

½ CUP COCONUT MILK

150 GRAMS TENDER-STEM BROCCOLI, HALVED CROSSWAYS

80 GRAMS RICOTTA CHEESE (OPTIONAL)

2 TABLESPOONS NUTRITIONAL YEAST OR FINELY GRATED PARMESAN CHEESE

JUICE AND ZEST OF ½ LEMON

Preheat the oven to 180 °C.

Place the mushrooms onto a roasting tray. Pour 1 tablespoon melted coconut oil over each mushroom. Sprinkle over the oregano and season with salt and pepper.

Place the chickpeas, garlic and rosemary onto another roasting tray, add the remaining tablespoon of melted coconut oil and toss until the chickpeas are evenly covered. Pop the trays of chickpeas and mushrooms into the oven and roast for 30 minutes until the chickpeas are crunchy and the garlic is soft. Depending on the size of the mushrooms, you can roast them for an additional 10 minutes. Once ready, remove from the oven.

Meanwhile, cook the pasta in salted water as per the packet instructions. Once ready, drain and drizzle with the olive oil and add the coconut milk. This will prevent the pasta from sticking together.

Boil the kettle and pour boiling water over the broccoli in a small bowl. Let it sit for 6 minutes, then drain and rinse in cold water.

Slice the mushrooms and add them to the pasta along with the garlic cloves and broccoli. Toss until well combined and then transfer to a large serving bowl or platter.

Serve topped with the crumbled ricotta (if using), crunchy chickpeas and a crack of black pepper. Sprinkle over the nutritional yeast or Parmesan, lemon juice and lemon zest.

BAKED

'CHEESY' CAULIFLOWER AND TOMATO

SERVES: **4** | PREPARATION TIME: **15** MINUTES | COOKING TIME: **65** MINUTES

I created this recipe out of wanting the comfort of the classic mac and cheese and cheesy cauliflower bakes from my childhood. The only difference is that this one comes with a vegan béchamel that packs all the flavour with none of the guilt. The sauce is a great tool to have in your arsenal and can cover most veggies in a bake, such as broccoli or butternut. The topping is so delicious that if you like it really saucy, just double the amount!

2 MEDIUM-SIZED HEADS CAULIFLOWER,
BROKEN INTO FLORETS
300 GRAMS CHERRY TOMATOES
1 CUP CHICKPEAS, COOKED (SEE PAGE 24)
1 TABLESPOON MELTED COCONUT OIL
1 TEASPOON GRATED FRESH NUTMEG
1 TEASPOON GARLIC FLAKES
¼ TEASPOON CAYENNE PEPPER
1 TABLESPOON FRESH THYME LEAVES
SALT AND PEPPER
1 SMALL HANDFUL FRESH PARSLEY
LEAVES (OPTIONAL)

'CHEESE' SAUCE

6 TABLESPOONS COCONUT OIL
6 TABLESPOONS SPELT FLOUR
2½ CUPS UNSWEETENED ALMOND MILK
¼ CUP NUTRITIONAL YEAST
½ TABLESPOON MAPLE SYRUP
SALT AND PEPPER

TOPPING

⅓ CUP DRIED BREADCRUMBS
2 TABLESPOONS OLIVE OIL
¼ TEASPOON GARLIC FLAKES
¼ TEASPOON RED CHILLI FLAKES

Preheat the oven to 180 °C.

Place the cauliflower florets, cherry tomatoes and chickpeas into a large casserole dish. Add the coconut oil, spices and thyme and season with salt and pepper. Toss until everything is evenly coated and pop it into the oven for 40 minutes, uncovered, or until golden brown. Once ready, remove from the oven, leaving the oven switched on.

For the sauce, heat the coconut oil in a small saucepan over medium heat. Add the spelt flour while whisking continuously, making sure there are no lumps. Cook for 4–5 minutes. Add the almond milk very slowly while whisking continuously. The sauce will begin to thicken, but don't stop whisking. Once the sauce is thick, fold through the nutritional yeast for that tasty cheese flavour. Add the maple syrup and season to taste, then remove from the heat.

For the topping, mix all the ingredients together in a small bowl.

Once the cauliflower is cooked, pour over the sauce until all the vegetables are covered. Top off with the breadcrumbs.

Pop the casserole dish back into the oven for 25 minutes, keeping an eye on it. You want the breadcrumbs to become golden and crunchy. Garnish with parsley (if using) and serve as a side or as the main affair with a delicious fresh salad to contrast the baked goodness.

KITCHARI

BROWN RICE AND SPICES

SERVES: 5 | PREPARATION TIME: 15 MINUTES *(EXCLUDING SOAKING)* | COOKING TIME: 40 MINUTES

Because this book has touched on Ayurveda, I thought a delicious kitchari would be a great recipe to include. Kitchari is a traditional Ayurvedic dish that is nourishing and gentle on the digestive system. It supports the balance of all three doshas. It is made with cooked lentils and rice with warming spices. Kitchari has subdued flavours so feel free to add more spices if you like. It's something I turn to when I don't feel well or when I feel like my digestion needs a break. It's also a great meal to have around your period or to use during a detox. Eat for breakfast, lunch and dinner over the space of three days, drinking only water and caffeine-free tea to gently detox the system and support gut healing.

½ CUP COCONUT YOGHURT

JUICE OF ½ LEMON

3 SMALL HANDFULS FRESH CORIANDER
   LEAVES, FINELY CHOPPED

SALT

200 GRAMS UNCOOKED SPLIT RED LENTILS
   OR MUNG BEANS

200 GRAMS UNCOOKED WILD OR
   BROWN RICE

1 THUMB-SIZE PIECE FRESH GINGER,
   PEELED AND GRATED

¼ CUP DESICCATED COCONUT

1½ TABLESPOONS GHEE OR COCONUT OIL

1 TEASPOON GROUND CUMIN

1 TEASPOON GROUND CORIANDER

½ TEASPOON YELLOW MUSTARD SEEDS

1 TEASPOON GROUND TURMERIC

1 TEASPOON FENNEL SEEDS

1 TEASPOON FENUGREEK SEEDS

1 TEASPOON GROUND CARDAMOM

1 TEASPOON GROUND CLOVES

1 TEASPOON GROUND BLACK PEPPER

1 TEASPOON GROUND CINNAMON

80 GRAMS RAW ALMONDS, ROASTED (SEE
   PAGE 24) AND CHOPPED (OPTIONAL)

Mix the yoghurt, lemon juice and one handful of the coriander together in a small bowl. Season with a little salt and set aside.

Soak the lentils and rice in a bowl of cold water for at least 1 hour. Rinse under cold running water until the water runs clear and ensure any stones are removed.

Place another handful of the fresh coriander, along with the ginger, desiccated coconut and 1 cup water into a high-speed blender and blend until smooth.

Heat the ghee or coconut oil in a medium-sized saucepan over medium heat. Add all the spices and mix well. Heat the spices for about 3 minutes until they release all their flavour and become aromatic. Add the rice and lentil mixture as well as 5 cups water and the coriander and coconut mixture. Bring to a simmer and cook for 35 minutes. If the water level drops too low too quickly, top it up. Once the rice has cooked and the water has been absorbed, remove from the heat. You want the consistency to be like porridge.

Serve topped with the remaining fresh coriander, a swirl of the yoghurt and a sprinkle of almonds (if using). Garnish with edible flowers, if desired.

MUSHROOM DUMPLINGS

WITH SESAME CRUST

SERVES: 2 | PREPARATION TIME: 30 MINUTES | COOKING TIME: 10 MINUTES

These dumplings are a little different and show how something as simple as a sesame crust can add a wow factor to a dish. They are light and fresh and incorporate all of the delicious Asian flavours you've come to expect from a dish like this. It has the spicy and the sweet, and the crunch of the sesame seeds leaves you with the ultimate satisfaction. Sesame seeds are a very good source of antioxidants, protein and B vitamins. Try incorporating them into your everyday meals by sprinkling them on your food or blending them into a dip.

3 TABLESPOONS COCONUT OIL

1 SMALL LEEK, FINELY SLICED

½ CARROT, SCRUBBED AND GRATED

2 CLOVES GARLIC, MINCED

1 TEASPOON RED CHILLI FLAKES

2 CUPS SHIMEJI OR EXOTIC MUSHROOMS,
   ROUGHLY CHOPPED

1 THUMB-SIZE PIECE FRESH GINGER,
   PEELED AND GRATED

1 CUP ROUGHLY CHOPPED PAK CHOI

2 TABLESPOONS LIQUID AMINOS OR
   SOY SAUCE

BLACK PEPPER

WONTON WRAPPERS

⅓ CUP WHITE SESAME SEEDS

2 SPRING ONIONS, FINELY SLICED

GINGER DIPPING SAUCE

JUICE OF 1 LIME

½ FRESH RED CHILLI, FINELY CHOPPED

5 TABLESPOONS LIQUID AMINOS

1 TEASPOON GRATED FRESH GINGER

2 TEASPOONS RAW HONEY

5 TABLESPOONS SESAME OIL

Mix together all the ingredients for the dipping sauce in a small bowl. Set aside.

Heat 1 tablespoon of the coconut oil in a medium-sized frying pan over medium heat. Once hot, add the leek, carrot, garlic and chilli flakes and sauté for 5 minutes, stirring often. Add the mushrooms and ginger and cook for a further 10 minutes. Once the mushrooms are cooked, add the pak choi and liquid aminos or soy sauce. Stir until well combined. Season with black pepper and then set aside.

Lay out the wonton wrappers on a flat surface. Spoon a slightly heaped teaspoon of the mushroom mixture into the middle of each wrapper. Using a brush or your finger, lightly coat the outer edges of the wrapper with a little water. Wrap the wonton by bringing up the edges and pinching them together to create a little crescent-shaped parcel.

Place the sesame seeds into a small bowl. Lightly coat the underside of the dumplings with a little water. Dunk the bottom of each dumpling into the sesame seeds, creating a solid sesame-crusted base.

Heat the remaining 2 tablespoons coconut oil in a medium-sized frying pan over medium heat. Once hot, add the dumplings and fill the pan so that they sit upright on their sesame-crusted bases. Fry the dumplings for about 4 minutes. Carefully (it will spatter) add ¼ cup water to the pan and cover with a lid for 5 minutes. This will steam the dumplings.

Serve sprinkled with spring onions and the dipping sauce on the side.

MUNG BEAN DHAL

WITH SWEET-AND-SOUR PINEAPPLE CHUTNEY

SERVES: 4 | PREPARATION TIME: 15 MINUTES | COOKING TIME: 1 HOUR

I encourage you to play around with combinations of cooked and raw foods. Raw foods mean that the original nutritional value is undisturbed by the heating process that comes with cooking. This means that you get the full health benefit. Pineapple is high in vitamins and offers a spicy dish the perfect sweetness.

DHAL

- 1 TABLESPOON COCONUT OIL
- 1 BROWN ONION, FINELY DICED
- 2 CLOVES GARLIC, MINCED
- 1 THUMB-SIZE PIECE FRESH GINGER, PEELED AND GRATED
- 2 FRESH GREEN CHILLIES, FINELY CHOPPED
- 2 TEASPOONS CUMIN SEEDS
- 2 TEASPOONS CORIANDER SEEDS OR GROUND CORIANDER
- 2 TEASPOONS GROUND TURMERIC
- 2 TEASPOONS GROUND CINNAMON
- 2 TABLESPOONS DESICCATED COCONUT
- 200 GRAMS UNCOOKED RED SPLIT LENTILS
- 250 GRAMS MUNG BEANS, SOAKED OVERNIGHT OR FOR AT LEAST 4 HOURS
- 2 CUPS VEGETABLE STOCK
- 2 CUPS WATER
- 400 MILLILITRES COCONUT MILK
- 2 HANDFULS BABY SPINACH
- SALT AND PEPPER
- 1 HANDFUL FRESH CORIANDER LEAVES
- 2 LIMES

PINEAPPLE CHUTNEY

- 1 TEASPOON COCONUT OIL
- ½ RED ONION, FINELY SLICED
- 1 CUP DICED FRESH PINEAPPLE
- 1 FRESH RED CHILLI, FINELY SLICED
- 1 FRESH JALAPEÑO CHILLI, FINELY SLICED
- ¼ CUP RAW WALNUTS, ROUGHLY CHOPPED
- 1 TEASPOON SALT
- 1 TEASPOON GROUND CUMIN
- ¼ TEASPOON GRATED FRESH NUTMEG
- PINCH OF GROUND CLOVES
- 1 CUP WHITE WINE VINEGAR
- ½ CUP COCONUT SUGAR

For the dhal, heat the coconut oil in a medium-sized saucepan over medium heat. Add the onion and sauté for 5 minutes, stirring often. Add the garlic and sauté for a further 5 minutes, then add the ginger and chillies.

While the onion is cooking, lightly toast the cumin and coriander seeds in a separate small pan over medium heat. Once ready, grind using a spice grinder or mortar and pestle. Add to the onion and sauté to release the flavours. Add the remaining spices and coconut and mix well.

Make sure the lentils and mung beans are well rinsed and that all stones are removed. Add the lentils and mung beans to the onion mixture and then add the stock, water and coconut milk to the saucepan. Bring to a simmer with the lid on and cook for 45 minutes, still covered, stirring every 10 minutes. If the liquid drops too low, top up with a little water – you want the mixture to become just firmer than porridge. Once the dhal is ready, switch off the heat and stir in the baby spinach so that it wilts. Season to taste.

While the dhal is cooking, prepare the chutney. Heat the coconut oil in a medium-sized frying pan over medium heat. Add the onion and sauté until translucent. Add the pineapple and chillies and sauté for a further 5 minutes. Add the walnuts and spices and mix well. Add the vinegar and sugar and bring to a slow simmer. Let this cook for the duration of the dhal. Once the liquid has been absorbed and the pineapple has cooked soft, the chutney is ready. Remove from the heat and let it cool. Store the chutney in a glass jar and use some for serving and some for later.

Once the dhal is ready, serve with a dollop of chutney, fresh coriander and a squeeze of lime. If desired, serve with naan bread or rotis.

COUNTRYSIDE

ASPARAGUS AND LEEK PIE

SERVES: 6 | PREPARATION TIME: 25 MINUTES | COOKING TIME: 35 MINUTES

Eating in silence means you're eating more mindfully, which is better for your health as you are able to tune into the sensations in your body. Leeks are a good source of vitamins C, A and K, and are a beautiful substitute for the traditionally used onion, which can aggravate the digestive system.

CRUST

1 ROLL PHYLLO PASTRY
7 TABLESPOONS OLIVE OIL

FILLING

2 TEASPOONS COCONUT OIL
1 CLOVE GARLIC, FINELY CHOPPED
1 TABLESPOON FRESH THYME LEAVES
⅓ CUP FRESH MINT LEAVES
¼ TEASPOON CAYENNE PEPPER
6 LEEKS, FINELY SLICED
1 CUP TENDER-STEM BROCCOLI, CHOPPED
100 GRAMS FRESH ASPARAGUS, ENDS
    REMOVED, CHOPPED
1 CUP FRESH OR FROZEN PEAS
2 TABLESPOONS SPELT FLOUR
1½ CUPS VEGETABLE STOCK
1 TABLESPOON LEMON ZEST
SALT AND PEPPER
3 TABLESPOONS RICOTTA CHEESE

TOPPING

½ CUP ROLLED OATS
¼ CUP PUMPKIN SEEDS
ZEST OF ½ LEMON
1 TABLESPOON FRESH THYME LEAVES
PINCH OF SALT
1 TABLESPOON OLIVE OIL

For the filling, heat the coconut oil in a medium-sized frying pan over medium heat. Add the garlic and sauté for 2 minutes. Add the thyme, mint and cayenne pepper and mix well. Add the leeks and cook for 10 minutes until they have softened. Add the broccoli, asparagus and peas and mix well. Add the spelt flour, vegetable stock and lemon zest and season to taste. Simmer for 10 minutes. Once the sauce starts to thicken, remove from the heat.

In the meantime, place all the ingredients for the topping into a food processor and pulse until crumbs form. Set aside.

Place the phyllo pastry sheets – one at a time – into a 24 cm pie dish, making sure to cover the base and that the edges overlap the dish by about 5 cm. Brush each layer completely with olive oil. This is an open pie, but the edges will become crunchy when baked. Work quickly as the phyllo can dry out and crack.

Preheat the oven to 180 °C.

Spoon the filling into the pie crust and dot with the ricotta. (Alternatively, when making the filling, leave some of the leeks and broccoli whole and arrange them in the pie crust as shown in the photograph.) Crumble over the topping and pop the pie into the oven. Bake for 35 minutes or until the edges of the pie are golden brown.

KINDNESS PAELLA

TEMPEH AND GREEN BEANS

SERVES: 4 | PREPARATION TIME: 15 MINUTES | COOKING TIME: 1 HOUR

Tempeh is a traditional Indonesian soya product that is made from fermented soya beans. You can find it at your local Asian supermarket or health store. It is naturally high in protein and can replace traditional protein in a meal. When it comes to new ingredients, take on the saying I learnt in Indonesia: 'Never try, never know!'

1 LARGE SWEET POTATO, SCRUBBED AND
   CUBED INTO BITE-SIZE PIECES
COCONUT OIL
SALT AND PEPPER
1½ CUPS UNCOOKED BROWN OR RED RICE
½ RED ONION, FINELY SLICED
2 CLOVES GARLIC, MINCED
1 TABLESPOON SMOKED PAPRIKA
2 TEASPOONS GROUND TURMERIC
1 TEASPOON CURRY POWDER
4 BAY LEAVES, FRESH OR DRIED, TORN
1 LARGE CARROT, SCRUBBED AND GRATED
500 GRAMS CHERRY TOMATOES
½ CUP PASSATA
½ CUP VEGETABLE STOCK
250 GRAMS TEMPEH, SLICED 5 MM THICK
2–3 LARGE COURGETTES, CUT INTO BITE-
   SIZE PIECES
350 GRAMS GREEN BEANS, TOPPED AND
   HALVED CROSSWAYS
ZEST AND JUICE OF 1 LEMON
80 GRAMS RAW ALMONDS, ROASTED (SEE
   PAGE 24) AND ROUGHLY CHOPPED

Preheat the oven to 180 °C.

Place the sweet potato cubes onto a roasting tray and add 2 teaspoons coconut oil. Toss until evenly covered, season with salt and pepper and pop them into the oven. Roast for 30 minutes or until golden brown and soft. Once ready, remove from the oven and set aside.

Cook the rice in salted water as per the packet instructions.

Heat 1 tablespoon coconut oil in a medium-sized saucepan or a deep frying pan over medium heat. Add the onion and sauté for roughly 5 minutes until translucent. Add the garlic and sauté for a further 2 minutes, stirring often. Add the spices and allow the heat to release the flavours while stirring. If the mixture sticks, add a tablespoon of water. Add the bay leaves, carrot and tomatoes and mix well. Add the passata and vegetable stock and bring the mixture to a simmer with the lid on. This sauce will be your base so you want to cook the acidity out of the tomatoes. Cook for roughly 35 minutes, stirring and checking on it throughout.

While the sauce is cooking you can fry the tempeh. Heat 1 tablespoon coconut oil in a medium-sized frying pan over medium to high heat. Once the oil is hot, add the slices of tempeh to the pan. Fry for about 3 minutes on each side until golden brown and crunchy. Once ready, remove from the pan and set aside.

Using the same pan, add the courgettes and green beans and fry for 5–10 minutes. You want them to still be crunchy but the raw taste must be cooked out.

When all of your elements are ready, it's time to combine them. Add the rice to the tomato base along with the sweet potatoes and greens. Mix well until combined and then cook for an additional 10 minutes. Add the lemon zest and season to taste.

Serve topped with the tempeh, a sprinkle of almonds and a squeeze of lemon. If preferred, stir the tempeh into the mix rather than serving it on top and garnish with fresh herbs of choice.

SPANAKOPITA

SPINACH, DILL AND FETA

SERVES: 6 | PREPARATION TIME: 15 MINUTES | COOKING TIME: 40 MINUTES

This is the perfect combination of crunch and melt-in-your-mouth creaminess. Originating from Greece, this dish is traditionally made with feta. If you are being mindful of your dairy intake, then I encourage you to try the vegan feta filling. Spinach is an excellent source of vitamins K, A and C as well as magnesium and iron. If you are anaemic, then this is the dish for you to pack in those missing nutrients.

2 TEASPOONS COCONUT OIL

2 MEDIUM-SIZED LEEKS, FINELY SLICED

2 CLOVES GARLIC, MINCED

500 GRAMS SWISS CHARD, CHOPPED

½ CUP FRESH DILL LEAVES, ROUGHLY
   CHOPPED

¼ CUP FRESH PARSLEY LEAVES, ROUGHLY
   CHOPPED

¼ CUP NUTRITIONAL YEAST

¼ TEASPOON CAYENNE PEPPER

BLACK PEPPER

1 ROLL PHYLLO PASTRY

⅓ CUP OLIVE OIL

1 TABLESPOON POPPY SEEDS

OPTION 1 (VEGAN FETA FILLING)

1 CUP RAW CASHEW NUTS, SOAKED
   OVERNIGHT OR FOR AT LEAST 4 HOURS
   IN WARM WATER

2 TABLESPOONS APPLE CIDER VINEGAR

1 TEASPOON SEA SALT

OPTION 2

5 EGGS

2 WHEELS FETA, CRUMBLED

Preheat the oven to 180 °C.

If you're going with the vegan feta option, place the soaked cashew nuts, vinegar and salt into a food processor and pulse until a feta-like crumb forms. Once ready, set aside.

Heat the coconut oil in a medium-sized frying pan over medium heat. Add the leeks and sauté for roughly 10 minutes until softened. Add the garlic and cook for a further 2 minutes. Remove the pan from the heat, then add the Swiss chard and herbs and fold through, letting the residual heat in the pan wilt the greens – you want the greens to wilt but you don't want them to be overcooked. Add the nutritional yeast and cayenne pepper and toss. Transfer the mixture to a large bowl.

If you are using eggs (non vegan), add them to the mixture along with the real feta. If not, skip the egg step and add the vegan feta. Season with black pepper and mix until well combined.

To assemble the spanakopita, place all the sheets of phyllo, one by one, into a 30 cm quiche dish so that the corners are randomly aligned. Fill the centre with the filling. One by one, fold the corners of each sheet into the middle while brushing the exposed areas generously with olive oil. Sprinkle over the poppy seeds and pop the dish into the oven. Bake for 35–40 minutes until the pastry is golden brown and crunchy. Garnish with micro herbs, if desired, and serve with a fresh garden salad as a main course, or as a side.

MEZZE FEAST

ROASTED MUSHROOMS WITH BUTTER BEAN PURÉE AND BEETROOT PARATHA

SERVES: 4 | PREPARATION TIME: 30 MINUTES *(EXCLUDING MARINATING TIME)* | COOKING TIME: 45 MINUTES

Mushrooms are the fruit of fungi. They are powerful healers in their own right and can offer a vast array of health properties, such as B vitamins and a powerful antioxidant called selenium, which helps to support the immune system and prevents damage to cells and tissues. This meal is one where I encourage you to let your creative flag fly. Explore what mushrooms are available at your local farmers' market or fresh produce section and go wild.

MUSHROOMS

- 2 PRESERVED LEMONS, FINELY CHOPPED AND SEEDS REMOVED
- 2 TEASPOONS GROUND CUMIN
- 2 TEASPOONS GROUND ALLSPICE
- 2 TEASPOONS SMOKED PAPRIKA
- 1 TEASPOON CHIPOTLE POWDER
- 4 CLOVES GARLIC
- SALT AND PEPPER TO TASTE
- 1 TABLESPOON MELTED COCONUT OIL
- 800 GRAMS ASSORTED MUSHROOMS (OYSTER, PORTOBELLO, LARGE BROWN)
- 1 RED PEPPER, SEEDED AND CUT INTO CHUNKS
- 1 RED ONION, QUARTERED
- 2 TABLESPOONS BALSAMIC REDUCTION

BEETROOT PARATHA

- 1 CUP WHOLE WHEAT SPELT FLOUR
- ½ CUP WHITE SPELT FLOUR
- 4 TEASPOONS OLIVE OIL, PLUS EXTRA
- ½ TEASPOON SALT
- ½ TEASPOON GROUND CUMIN
- ¾ CUP COOKED BEETROOT

BUTTER BEAN PURÉE

- 250 GRAMS BUTTER BEANS, COOKED (SEE PAGE 24)
- 1 CLOVE GARLIC
- JUICE AND ZEST OF ½ LEMON
- ¼ CUP OLIVE OIL
- SALT AND PEPPER

SALSA

400 GRAMS CHERRY TOMATOES,
　QUARTERED
¼ RED ONION, FINELY SLICED
JUICE OF ½ LEMON
1 GENEROUS HANDFUL FRESH FLAT-LEAF
　PARSLEY LEAVES, FINELY CHOPPED
1 TABLESPOON APPLE CIDER VINEGAR
SALT AND PEPPER

DUKKHA CRUNCH

80 GRAMS RAW HAZELNUTS
2 TEASPOONS CUMIN SEEDS
1 TEASPOON GROUND WHITE PEPPER
2 TEASPOONS CORIANDER SEEDS
½ TEASPOON SALT
1 TEASPOON PAPRIKA
1 TEASPOON FENNEL SEEDS
3 TABLESPOONS SUNFLOWER SEEDS
1½ TABLESPOONS SESAME SEEDS

TO SERVE

½ CUCUMBER, SLICED INTO ROUNDS
6 RADISHES, THINLY SLICED INTO ROUNDS
¼ CUP TAHINI
OLIVE OIL
SALT AND PEPPER

To make the marinade for the mushrooms, place the preserved lemons, spices, garlic, salt and pepper and melted coconut oil into a food processor. Give it about six pulses so that it is still slightly chunky – you want a muddled mixture.

Gently mix the mushrooms, red pepper and onion into the marinade in an airtight container and set aside in the fridge for at least 2 hours or overnight if possible.

Preheat the oven to 200 °C.

Place the mushroom mixture into a large roasting dish. Roast for 35–40 minutes until juicy and tender, tossing at the halfway mark. Drizzle over the balsamic reduction about 3 minutes before they are done to give them a pop of sweetness.

While the mushrooms are roasting, prepare the paratha (flatbreads). Mix the flours, olive oil, salt and cumin in a large mixing bowl. Blend the beetroot until smooth in a high-speed food processor. If it gets stuck you can add a tablespoon of water. Add the beetroot purée to the flour mixture and mix until well combined and a dough forms. If the mixture is too stiff, you can add a little more water. You want a non-sticky dough. Let the dough rest for 15 minutes.

Divide the dough into six balls. Roll out each ball into a flatbread shape. Lightly oil each side of the paratha and place in a griddle pan over high heat. Grill for 4 minutes on each side or until the grill marks have formed and the bread has bubbled. Once ready, pop it on a plate until ready for serving. Repeat with the remaining parathas.

For the butter bean purée, combine all the ingredients in a food processor and blend until smooth. Season to taste.

For the salsa, mix together all the ingredients in a small bowl, season to taste and set aside.

For the dukkha crunch, toast the nuts in a small frying pan over medium heat for about 2 minutes, then remove them from the pan. Roughly roll the hazelnuts in your hands to remove some of the skins.

Add all the spices and seeds, except the sesame seeds, to the same frying pan and toast for about 2 minutes over medium heat until the flavour is released. Transfer the spices and seeds to a pestle and mortar and crush finely. Add the hazelnuts and roughly bash them in as well. Mix in the sesame seeds and set aside.

To assemble your plate, start with a warm flatbread, smear on a generous dollop of butter bean purée followed by the mushroom mix. Top with salsa, cucumber and radishes, sprinkle over some dukkha crunch and drizzle with tahini and olive oil. Add a crack of salt and black pepper and garnish as desired.

DECADENT CURRY

CHICKPEA AND SWEET POTATO

SERVES: 4 | PREPARATION TIME: 15 MINUTES | COOKING TIME: 50 MINUTES

A curry spice blend is rich in anti-inflammatory compounds and enjoying it liberally can boost heart health, reduce oxidative stress and improve blood sugar levels. The best part of it is not just the health benefits, but also the fact that it's simply delicious.

1 TABLESPOON COCONUT OIL

1 TEASPOON YELLOW MUSTARD SEEDS

1 BROWN ONION, DICED

2 CLOVES GARLIC, MINCED

2 TEASPOONS CURRY POWDER

1 TEASPOON GROUND CUMIN

1 TEASPOON GROUND CORIANDER

½–1 TEASPOON CAYENNE PEPPER

1 TABLESPOON GARAM MASALA

1 TEASPOON GROUND CINNAMON

200 GRAMS CHERRY TOMATOES, HALVED

250 GRAMS CHICKPEAS, COOKED (SEE
    PAGE 24)

1 LARGE SWEET POTATO, SCRUBBED
    AND CUBED

4 CUPS VEGETABLE STOCK

½ CUP UNCOOKED RED RICE

400 MILLILITRES COCONUT MILK

SALT AND PEPPER

1 GENEROUS HANDFUL SWISS CHARD,
    FINELY CHOPPED

TO SERVE

1 CUP PLAIN YOGHURT

1 HANDFUL FRESH CORIANDER LEAVES,
    ROUGHLY CHOPPED

ZEST OF 1 LEMON

JUICE OF ½ LEMON

80–100 GRAMS RAW ALMONDS, ROASTED
    (SEE PAGE 24) AND ROUGHLY CHOPPED

Heat the coconut oil in a medium-sized saucepan over medium heat. Add the mustard seeds and fry until they start to pop. Once they start popping, add the onion and sauté for 5 minutes until translucent. Add the garlic and sauté for a further 2 minutes.

Add all the spices and sauté for 1 minute until aromatic. If it sticks, add a tablespoon of water to help it along.

Add the tomatoes, chickpeas, sweet potato and vegetable stock and simmer for 15–20 minutes, stirring often. If it gets a bit dry, top up with water and mix well. Give your curry some love and check on it often.

Add the rice and coconut milk to the saucepan and continue simmering for another 30 minutes. Season to taste with a generous crack of salt and some black pepper.

Once the sweet potato is soft and the rice is cooked, your curry is ready. Stir in the Swiss chard and spoon the curry into bowls. Top with a swirl of yoghurt, coriander, lemon zest and juice and a sprinkling of almonds.

VEGGIE CASSEROLE

WITH SPINACH AND CASHEW CREAM

SERVES: 4 | PREPARATION TIME: 15 MINUTES | COOKING TIME: 1 HOUR 10 MINUTES

I love veggie bakes, and I love using as many veggies together as possible in one dish. A veggie bake offers a vast array of nutrients that are not only good for your health, but also satiate you so that you aren't opening your snacking cupboard looking for crisps half an hour after eating a meal. Variety is key in healthy eating as well as plant-based eating.

2 RED ONIONS, FINELY SLICED

500 GRAMS CHERRY TOMATOES, HALVED

1 TABLESPOON MELTED COCONUT OIL

1 TEASPOON RED CHILLI FLAKES

ZEST OF 1 LEMON

SALT AND PEPPER

600 GRAMS BABY POTATOES, SCRUBBED

2 MEDIUM-SIZED AUBERGINES, SLICED
    INTO 5 MM THICK ROUNDS

5 TABLESPOONS OLIVE OIL

1 TEASPOON DRIED OREGANO

1 TEASPOON PAPRIKA

300 GRAMS TENDER-STEM BROCCOLI,
    STALKS TRIMMED OFF, HALVED
    CROSSWAYS

2 HANDFULS KALE, STALKS REMOVED AND
    LEAVES FINELY CHOPPED

½ CUP PUMPKIN SEEDS, TOASTED (SEE
    PAGE 24)

SPINACH CASHEW CREAM

1 CUP RAW CASHEW NUTS, SOAKED IN
    WARM WATER OVERNIGHT OR FOR AT
    LEAST 4 HOURS

1 HANDFUL BABY SPINACH

2 CLOVES GARLIC

JUICE OF ½ LEMON

¼ TEASPOON CAYENNE PEPPER

1 TABLESPOON NUTRITIONAL YEAST

1 TABLESPOON OLIVE OIL

Preheat the oven to 200 °C.

Place the onions and tomatoes onto a large baking tray and toss them with the coconut oil. Sprinkle over the chilli flakes, add the lemon zest and season with salt and pepper. Pop the tray into the oven and roast for 30 minutes until the tomatoes are golden and gooey. (Leave the oven switched on, as you'll need to roast the potatoes a bit later too.)

Meanwhile, add the potatoes to a large saucepan of salted boiling water and boil for 12–15 minutes until tender when pierced with a fork. You don't want to overcook them so that they are too soft. Once cooked through, drain and set aside.

While the potatoes are cooking, heat a griddle pan over medium heat until hot and then add the aubergines. Cook for 2–3 minutes per side until charred. You'll need to do this in batches. Once they are ready, pop them onto a plate, drizzle with 2 tablespoons of the olive oil and season with salt and pepper.

Place the boiled potatoes into a deep roasting dish and squash them flat with the back of a fork, forming a solid layer. Drizzle with the remaining 3 tablespoons olive oil, sprinkle with the oregano and paprika and season with salt and pepper. Pop the potatoes into the oven and roast for 15 minutes while you make the cashew cream.

For the cashew cream, add the cashew nuts and 3 tablespoons of the soaking water to a food processor and blend until smooth. Add the remaining ingredients and blend until you get a thick creamy sauce. You can add an extra tablespoon olive oil to help it along if need be.

Now you are ready to assemble your veggie bake. Remove the potatoes from the oven and add an even layer of the broccoli on top. Sprinkle the kale over the broccoli to create the next layer. Overlap the aubergines for the next layer. Add the tomatoes and onions and smooth them out with the back of a wooden spoon, making sure all the veggies are covered.

Pour the cashew cream over the tomato layer and spread out evenly. Season to taste with salt and pepper and pop the bake into the oven for 30–35 minutes until bubbling and golden on top.

Top with the toasted pumpkin seeds and a crack of black pepper and serve.

ULTIMATE VEGGIE CURRY

BUTTER CHICKPEA AND TOFU

SERVES: 4 | PREPARATION TIME: 15 MINUTES | COOKING TIME: 40 MINUTES

Tofu is made from fermented soya beans, and you can find it at Asian supermarkets or your local health store. For this recipe, I recommend buying a GMO-free, firmer tofu as you want to fry it up so that it gets crispy. Not all tofu is created equal, so try them out and find the one that works best for you. Tofu will take on the flavour of what you cook it in, so although it can be perceived as bland if not cooked correctly, it can also be absolutely incredible when submerged in surrounding flavours. It is also naturally high in protein and a wonderul substitute for many meat products.

1 CUP UNCOOKED BROWN RICE

2 TABLESPOONS COCONUT OIL

250 GRAMS TOFU (OR PANEER), CUBED

¾ CUP RAW CASHEW NUTS, ROASTED (SEE PAGE 24)

1¾ CUPS COCONUT MILK

3 TABLESPOONS TOMATO PASTE

¼ CUP GREEK YOGHURT OR COCONUT CREAM

½ RED ONION, DICED

2 CLOVES GARLIC, MINCED

1 TABLESPOON GRATED FRESH GINGER

2 TEASPOONS CURRY POWDER

3 TABLESPOONS MASSAMAN OR RED CURRY PASTE

2 TABLESPOONS GARAM MASALA

2 TEASPOONS GROUND TURMERIC

1 TEASPOON CAYENNE PEPPER (OR TO TASTE)

½ TEASPOON SALT

250 GRAMS CHICKPEAS, COOKED (SEE PAGE 24)

250 GRAMS TENDER-STEM BROCCOLI

1 HANDFUL FRESH CORIANDER LEAVES, ROUGHLY CHOPPED

Cook the rice as per the packet instructions. Once the water has evaporated, remove from the heat and set aside with the lid on to steam.

Heat 1 tablespoon of the coconut oil in a medium-sized frying pan over medium heat. Add the tofu and cook for roughly 3 minutes per side until crispy. Once ready, remove from the heat, drain on paper towel and set aside.

Place the roasted cashew nuts, coconut milk, tomato paste, yoghurt or coconut cream and ½ cup water into a food processor or blender and blend until smooth. Set aside.

Using the same frying pan from the tofu, heat the remaining tablespoon of coconut oil over medium heat. Once hot, add the onion and sauté for 5 minutes until translucent. Add the garlic and ginger and cook for another 5 minutes until the onion starts to caramelise.

Add the curry powder, curry paste, garam masala, turmeric, cayenne pepper and salt and cook for another minute to release the fragrance of the spices. Once ready, pour in the cashew sauce and mix well. Bring the sauce to a gentle simmer and cook for 15 minutes. If the sauce becomes too thick, add a little water to help it along.

Once the flavours have developed, stir in the tofu and the chickpeas and cook for 5 minutes. Stir in the broccoli and continue cooking for 5 minutes.

Serve a generous ladle of curry with a helping of rice or naan bread and top with fresh coriander leaves and a crack of black pepper.

HEALTHY SNACKING AND QUICK SIMPLE MEALS

This is the chapter that I suspect will get the most attention simply because time is of the essence. These meals are quick to put together and illustrate that it doesn't have to be time consuming to be healthy or create something tasty.

But you are worth taking the time to prepare your meal with love, no matter how long it takes. Change your thinking here and now. Tell yourself that you are worthy of finding balance, eating healthy nourishing food that will fuel your body with energy, a clear mind and better sleep. If you aren't sure if you believe it yet, that is okay. Fake it till you make it. We all have moments of self-doubt and criticism. How we navigate those stormy waters can boost our self-confidence. Acknowledge yourself and your value in the space of your life, your work, your family and your friends. You are loved and I want you to let that shine. The path that you have walked is not without reason. Every moment in your life has led you up to this point of healing.

- When last did you feel your best?

- What did you say to yourself or tell yourself at that point?

- Why did that feeling end? What was happening at that stage?

HEALTH TIPS
- Get rid of the soft drinks and sugary fruit juices! Even the diet ones. They are filled with chemicals and the diet drinks trick the body into thinking that it is getting sugar, which can cause more havoc than the sugar itself. Replace these drinks with sparkling water or 100 per cent pomegranate juice or tuck into one of the many herbal teas out there!
- Eat foods naturally high in antioxidants. How do you know if they are high in antioxidants? They are naturally intense in colour, such as blueberries, strawberries, red cabbage and butternut! Tuck into them all and get curious about the vegetables and fruits out there.
- Foods naturally high in vitamin C are not only good for your immune system, but also very good for a glowing skin. Lemons, oranges, peppers, broccoli and strawberries are all naturally filled with this glorious vitamin.

CRUNCHY CHICKPEAS

SPICY AND GOLDEN

SERVES: 2 | PREPARATION TIME: 5 MINUTES | COOKING TIME: 20–30 MINUTES

Simply add to salads, use as a topping on toast or enjoy as is as a snack.

200 GRAMS CHICKPEAS, COOKED (SEE PAGE 24)
1 TABLESPOON COCONUT OIL
½–1 TEASPOON CAYENNE PEPPER
¼ TEASPOON GROUND TURMERIC
1 TABLESPOON NUTRITIONAL YEAST (OPTIONAL)

Preheat the oven to 180 °C.

Rinse, drain and pat dry the chickpeas. Pop them into a roasting tray along with the coconut oil, cayenne pepper and turmeric. Toss everything together until the chickpeas are evenly covered. Pop the tray into the oven and roast for 20–30 minutes (depending on how crunchy you like them), tossing the chickpeas at the halfway mark. Five minutes before the chickpeas are ready to come out the oven, sprinkle over the nutritional yeast (if using) and pop the tray back into the oven. Once ready, remove from the oven and allow to cool. Store in an airtight container.

CARAMEL CRUNCH

SPICY ORANGE AND CARAMEL POPCORN

SERVES: **2** | PREPARATION TIME: **10** MINUTES | COOKING TIME: **15** MINUTES

Caramel popcorn is something that takes me back to my childhood. It is the ultimate combination of salty and sweet. Popcorn is exceptionally high in fibre and is a quick, easy snack that leaves you satisfied and keeps your inner child smiling. This version is slightly more indulgent than just your regular popcorn, but I guess that's part of the fun too. Orange peels are high in vitamins C and B6, and calcium, and I like to think that's what you're sprinkling over this indulgence.

1 TABLESPOON COCONUT OIL
½ CUP POPCORN KERNELS
1 TEASPOON MALDON SALT

CARAMEL

¾ CUP MAPLE SYRUP OR HONEY
½ CUP COCONUT CREAM SOLID (SEE PAGE 189)
JUICE OF ½ ORANGE
2 TABLESPOONS CASHEW NUT BUTTER OR ALMOND BUTTER
¼ TEASPOON CAYENNE PEPPER
½ TEASPOON SALT
ZEST OF 1 ORANGE

Heat the coconut oil in a medium-sized saucepan over medium to high heat. Once hot, add the popcorn kernels. Put the lid on and keep it on until all the kernels have popped. I usually swirl the kernels around, keeping the lid on, to allow all the kernels to be coated with the oil. I repeat this swirl action when half of the kernels have popped to make sure that the remaining kernels move to the bottom of the saucepan. When all the kernels have popped, remove from the heat and transfer into a large bowl.

Meanwhile, place the maple syrup or honey, the solid coconut cream and the orange juice into a medium-sized saucepan over medium to high heat. Bring the mixture to a boil and boil for 15 minutes, stirring often. The mixture should start to thicken and darken, forming the caramel sauce. Once this happens, remove it from the heat and stir in the cashew or almond butter, cayenne pepper and salt. Cool slightly before pouring the caramel over the popcorn and adding the orange zest. Toss the popcorn immediately with a fork so that the hot caramel evenly coats the popcorn. Allow to cool, sprinkle over some Maldon salt (and a little more orange zest, if desired) and then tuck in!

BUCKWHEAT NOODLES

MUSHROOMS, PAK CHOI AND EDAMAME

SERVES: 2 | PREPARATION TIME: 10 MINUTES | COOKING TIME: 10 MINUTES

This is the dish you can turn to when you haven't eaten lunch and you get home, you're starving, you want to make a bad food decision because you're craving the most nutrient-dense, carbohydrate meal, and then you feel overwhelmed by having to still prepare and cook, because it will take too long to feed your hunger. This light meal is hearty and comforting without taking too much time to make. Pak choi is high in folate, which plays a role in the production and repair of our DNA. This is true for most greens. Eating pak choi means you're also getting a higher dose of vitamins C and E, and betacarotene. It is one of the healthiest foods you can find, and sautéing it is my recommended method.

120 GRAMS BUCKWHEAT NOODLES

OLIVE OIL

3 TABLESPOONS LIQUID AMINOS OR
   SOY SAUCE

1 TABLESPOON RICE WINE VINEGAR

1 TABLESPOON HONEY

½ TABLESPOON COCONUT OIL

1 CARROT, SCRUBBED AND THINLY SLICED
   INTO ROUNDS

12 SHIITAKE MUSHROOMS, THICKLY
   SLICED

1 TABLESPOON GRATED FRESH GINGER

2 CUPS PACKED ROUGHLY CHOPPED
   PAK CHOI

1 SPRING ONION, FINELY SLICED, PLUS
   EXTRA FOR GARNISHING

1 TEASPOON SESAME OIL

½ CUP FROZEN OR FRESH EDAMAME
   BEANS (OPTIONAL)

2 TEASPOONS SESAME SEEDS

30 GRAMS MIXED SPROUTS

Cook the buckwheat noodles as per the packet instructions. Once ready, rinse under cold water and set aside. I like to drizzle over some olive oil to prevent the noodles from sticking together.

Place the liquid aminos, rice wine vinegar and honey into a small jar. Shake until well combined. Set aside.

Heat a medium-sized pan or wok over medium to high heat. Add the coconut oil. Once hot, add the carrot and cook for about 3 minutes. Add the mushrooms and cook for another 3 minutes. Add the ginger, pak choi and spring onion, stir well and cook for 3 minutes.

Add the noodles, rice vinegar mixture, sesame oil and edamame beans (if using) to the wok. Gently toss until well combined.

Serve topped with the sesame seeds, sprouts and some extra spring onion.

GRILLED BROCCOLI

WITH MUSHROOMS AND HALLOUMI

SERVES: **4** | PREPARATION TIME: **10** MINUTES | COOKING TIME: **20** MINUTES

Sometimes in life, you have to take the victories. Does this recipe have dairy in it? Yes. But it also has two heads of broccoli. Making this dish for your family might get you one step closer to having your children feast on some greens and enjoy it. Broccoli has bioactive compounds which have been shown to reduce inflammation in your body's tissues. It also contains high levels of calcium and vitamin K, both of which are important for bone health and prevention of osteoporosis. Moving your body daily in a gentle, loving way can also be the difference between growing old and getting old. This is when you see how important the synergy between food and movement is.

2 SMALL HEADS BROCCOLI, SLICED
    INTO STEAKS

3 TABLESPOONS OLIVE OIL

2 LARGE BROWN MUSHROOMS,
    THICKLY SLICED

6 SPRIGS FRESH SAGE OR THYME LEAVES

200 GRAMS HALLOUMI, SLICED (OR
    FIRM TOFU)

1 TABLESPOON MELTED COCONUT OIL

1 TEASPOON DRIED OREGANO

SALT AND PEPPER

80 GRAMS RAW ALMONDS,
    CHOPPED (OPTIONAL)

1 FRESH RED CHILLI, FINELY CHOPPED
    (OPTIONAL)

LEEKS

1 TABLESPOON COCONUT OIL

2 LEEKS, SLICED

1 TABLESPOON MAPLE SYRUP

½–1 TEASPOON CAYENNE PEPPER

1 TABLESPOON APPLE CIDER VINEGAR

Bring a griddle pan to a medium to high heat. Lay the broccoli steaks and mushrooms flat on a plate and lightly coat with the olive oil. Pop the broccoli steaks into the griddle pan and grill on each side for 5 minutes. For the last 3 minutes of cooking add 2 tablespoons water to the griddle pan and pop a lid on it. This allows the broccoli to steam gently while getting all the grill flavour. Once the steaks are ready, place them on the serving dish. Next, grill the mushrooms by popping them into the griddle pan and allowing them to cook for roughly 2–3 minutes on each side. Make sure the mushrooms are cooked through (taste them to make sure). Once ready, add them to the serving dish, along with the sage or thyme.

At the same time in a separate frying pan, fry the halloumi in the coconut oil until it is golden brown on each side, roughly 2 minutes per side. Season with oregano, salt and pepper. Once ready, top the mushrooms and broccoli with the cheese.

For the leeks, heat the coconut oil in a medium-sized frying pan over medium heat. Add the leeks and sauté them, stirring often, for 5 minutes. Add the maple syrup and cayenne pepper. Once the leeks are caramelised, after roughly 3 minutes, remove from the heat and add the apple cider vinegar. Stir until well combined.

Cover the broccoli, mushrooms and halloumi with the leeks. Top off with the almonds (if using), a crack of black pepper and a sprinkling of chopped chilli if you are craving some heat!

TOAST PARTY

A SNACK AFFAIR

SERVES: 2 | PREPARATION TIME: 10 MINUTES | COOKING TIME: 10 MINUTES

Almost anything goes well with a slice of toast! It's the perfect meal to have by yourself and it's even better when shared with a loved one.

2 SLICES SOURDOUGH, TOASTED TO YOUR
LIKING. IF YOU WANT TO MAKE YOUR
OWN, SEE PAGE 42.

PEANUT BUTTER AND BANANA

1–2 TABLESPOONS PURE PEANUT BUTTER
OR NUT BUTTER OF YOUR CHOICE
1 BANANA, SLICED INTO ROUNDS
¼ TEASPOON GROUND CINNAMON
1 TEASPOON MAPLE SYRUP
1 TEASPOON CHIA SEEDS

ARTICHOKE, GHERKIN AND RED PEPPER

2 TABLESPOONS OLIVE OIL
1 SMALL HANDFUL ROCKET
200 GRAMS MARINATED ARTICHOKE
HEARTS, ROUGHLY CHOPPED
4 MEDIUM-SIZED GHERKINS, SLICED
1 RED PEPPER (MARINATED, SAUTÉED
OR RAW)
SALT AND PEPPER

MUSHROOMS AND ROSEMARY

1 TEASPOON COCONUT OIL
150 GRAMS PORTOBELLO MUSHROOMS,
SLICED
1 TABLESPOON FINELY CHOPPED FRESH
ROSEMARY LEAVES
SALT AND PEPPER
HUMMUS (SEE PAGE 149)
1 SMALL HANDFUL BABY SPINACH
CRUNCHY CHICKPEAS (SEE PAGE 149)
JUICE OF ½ LEMON

BEETROOT, GOAT'S CHEESE AND ROCKET

2 TABLESPOONS OLIVE OIL
100 GRAMS CHEVIN GOAT'S MILK CHEESE
1 HANDFUL ROCKET
2 BEETROOTS, COOKED AND SLICED
JUICE AND ZEST OF ½ LEMON
30 GRAMS SUNFLOWER SEEDS
BLACK PEPPER

PEANUT BUTTER AND BANANA TOPPING

Smear the toast with peanut butter (in my world, the more the better; moderation can sometimes take a backseat). Cover the peanut butter with the banana slices, sprinkle with cinnamon, drizzle with maple syrup and top with chia seeds.

ARTICHOKE, GHERKIN AND RED PEPPER TOPPING

Drizzle the olive oil onto the toast. Layer with rocket, artichokes, gherkins and red pepper. Season to taste and serve.

MUSHROOM AND ROSEMARY TOPPING

Heat the coconut oil in a small frying pan over high heat. Add the mushrooms and sauté for 5 minutes, stirring often. Add the rosemary and sauté for an additional 2 minutes. Season with salt and pepper and remove from the heat.

Smear the hummus generously onto the toast, don't be shy. Top with the baby spinach, sautéed mushrooms, another dollop of hummus and the chickpeas. Drizzle with some lemon and you are good to go!

BEETROOT, GOAT'S CHEESE AND ROCKET TOPPING

Drizzle the olive oil over the toast. Smear on the goat's cheese as thick as you like it. Top with the rocket and beetroot slices. Add another drizzle of olive oil and a squeeze of lemon, and then top with lemon zest, sunflower seeds and a generous crack of black pepper.

For all these toast toppings, garnish as desired.

BLISS BALLS

CARDAMOM AND CRANBERRY

MAKES: 20 | PREPARATION TIME: 20 MINUTES

Being healthy needs to be easy and fun. If it isn't, then you aren't going to want to embrace it. These bliss balls are all about both. They are fun to make with a loved one or therapeutic to make alone. They will set you up to succeed because they count as meal prep (see page 21) and can support the stabilisation of blood sugar. This means you will move away from the insatiable hunger that drives you to inhale everything when you open the fridge door. Rather reach for one of these and enjoy it with a cup of tea.

BLISS BALLS

- 2 CUPS RAW WALNUTS
- 3 CUPS ALMOND FLOUR
- 9 MEDJOOL DATES, PITTED
- ½ CUP MELTED COCONUT OIL
- 2 TEASPOONS COCONUT FLOUR
- 2 TEASPOONS VANILLA PASTE
- 1 TEASPOON GROUND CARDAMOM
- 1 TEASPOON GROUND CINNAMON
- ¼ TEASPOON SALT
- 2 TEASPOONS REISHI OR MACA POWDER (OPTIONAL)
- 2 TABLESPOONS DRIED CRANBERRIES

COATING OPTIONS

- ½ CUP DESICCATED COCONUT OR A CRUSHED NUT OF YOUR CHOICE
- ¼ CUP BLACK SESAME SEEDS
- ¼ CUP WHITE SESAME SEEDS
- ¼ CUP MORINGA POWDER
- ¼ CUP RAW CACAO POWDER

Place all the ingredients for the bliss balls into a food processor or blender and blend until well combined and a dough forms. Use a tablespoon to scoop out the dough and roll into balls using your palms. I roll mine just bigger than a ping-pong ball. Roll the sticky balls in the coating(s) of your choice.

Store in an airtight container in the fridge or freezer. They will keep in the fridge for about 4 days and in the freezer for 2 months.

FLOWER ROLLS

WITH GINGER PEANUT DIPPING SAUCE

SERVES: 4 | PREPARATION TIME: 20 MINUTES | COOKING TIME: 10 MINUTES

If we become mindful of food and see it as a fundamental energy supply, and tune into our bodies and the way it makes us feel, then we will experience exactly that, the energy it offers us. If you have a sluggish digestive system, raw food can cause it to work harder and can leave you feeling bloated. These rolls are light on the digestive system and provide lots of fibre.

FLOWER ROLLS

- 1 AVOCADO, PEELED, PIP REMOVED, THINLY SLICED
- ½ MEDIUM-SIZED CUCUMBER, JULIENNED
- 1 MANGO OR PINEAPPLE, PEELED AND JULIENNED
- 1 CARROT, PEELED AND JULIENNED
- ¼ SMALL RED CABBAGE, THINLY SLICED
- ¼ CUP FRESH MINT LEAVES, ROUGHLY CHOPPED
- ¼ CUP FRESH CORIANDER LEAVES, ROUGHLY CHOPPED
- 200 GRAMS FIRM TOFU, JULIENNED
- 3 TABLESPOONS LIQUID AMINOS
- 1 PACKET VERMICELLI NOODLES
- 1 TABLESPOON RICE WINE VINEGAR
- 1 PACKET RICE PAPER WRAPPERS
- 1 PUNNET EDIBLE FLOWERS

GINGER PEANUT DIPPING SAUCE

- 1 TABLESPOON COCONUT OIL
- 1 THUMB-SIZE PIECE FRESH GINGER, PEELED AND GRATED
- 1 CLOVE GARLIC
- ½ CUP PURE PEANUT BUTTER
- ½–1 FRESH JALAPEÑO OR CHILLI OF YOUR CHOICE
- ZEST AND JUICE OF 1 LIME
- 2 TEASPOONS COCONUT SUGAR
- 3 TABLESPOONS WARM WATER

For the flower rolls, prep all of the vegetables and herbs and put them into separate small bowls for easy assembly. You can assemble the rolls ahead of time and keep them in the fridge or you can set out the bowls at a dinner party and guests can assemble their own rolls.

After cutting the tofu, toss it in 2 tablespoons of the liquid aminos so it can absorb the flavours. Set aside.

Place the noodles into a large bowl, cover with boiling water and soak for 5 minutes. Drain the noodles and pop them back into the bowl. Toss them in the rice wine vinegar and remaining 1 tablespoon liquid aminos. Set aside.

To make the sauce, heat the coconut oil in a medium-sized frying pan over medium heat. Add the ginger and garlic and sauté for 5 minutes, stirring often. Add the peanut butter and allow it to soften. Once ready, remove from the heat and pour the mixture into a high-speed blender. Add the remaining sauce ingredients, except the water, and blend until smooth. Add the water one spoon at a time until you have reached the desired consistency. Once ready, place in a small bowl and set aside.

To assemble the rolls, fill a roasting tray or similar dish with boiling water. If it cools during rolling, refill the water. Working with one wrapper at a time, place the rice paper wrapper flat in the water. Let it soften for 1–2 minutes. Once ready, carefully remove from the water, allowing excess water to drip off. Place the paper on a flat surface such as a plate. Place the edible flowers in a row in the middle, usually 4–5 flowers, followed by the variety of vegetables, herbs and tofu. Don't overfill the rolls. You want to leave a 1.5 cm gap along the edges and a 2 cm gap at the bottom and top of the roll. When closing the roll, fold the bottom and then the top over the contents. Holding this in place, roll up from one side to the other, making sure to tuck in the food as you roll. Repeat until all the rolls are made.

Arrange on a platter and garnish as desired. Best served fresh with the dipping sauce for dunking and at a dinner party with lots of laughter.

HEALING HUMMUS

RAINBOW SNACK PLATTER

SERVES: 4–6 | PREPARATION TIME: 20 MINUTES | COOKING TIME: 30 MINUTES

A chickpea is such a humble ingredient with the ability to be as adaptable as a chameleon. A great lesson for us to take on in our lives. Hummus is my go-to recipe – I make a batch at least once a week and eat it with vegetables (raw and roasted) or just on toast with some greens. It's a safety net to make sure that I have something quick to eat that is good for me. A great way to turn it into something more spectacular is to serve it with this rainbow platter. There is a vast variety of amazing fruits and vegetables available. Each one offers a new flavour, texture and nutritional value. Let your creativity flow and choose the amount you need to fill your platter. I treat the ingredients with integrity and either serve them raw, blanched or roasted. When I roast the vegetables, I use just enough coconut oil to coat them and add salt and pepper or fun spices such as turmeric and paprika. Roast the veg until soft, gooey and golden.

HUMMUS

- 250 GRAMS CHICKPEAS, COOKED (SEE PAGE 24)
- 2 TABLESPOONS TAHINI
- 7 TABLESPOONS OLIVE OIL
- 1 CLOVE GARLIC, PEELED
- ½ TEASPOON GRATED FRESH TURMERIC OR 1 TEASPOON GROUND TURMERIC
- ½ TEASPOON GRATED FRESH GINGER
- ¼ TEASPOON CAYENNE PEPPER
- 1 LEMON, JUICED
- SALT AND PEPPER

For the hummus, place all the ingredients into a blender and blend until smooth. Season to taste.

Serve with a rainbow selection of vegetables and fruits, as suggested below, and garnish as desired.

RAINBOW PLATTER IDEAS:

RED

- STRAWBERRIES, HALVED
- BEETROOT, BOILED AND THEN PEELED
- RED PEPPER, SEEDED AND SLICED
- RADISHES, SOME SLICED AND SOME SERVED WHOLE
- ROSA TOMATOES, HALVED
- RASPBERRIES
- GUAVAS, SLICED

PURPLE

- RED CABBAGE, SLICED
- PURPLE FIGS, SOME HALVED AND SOME SERVED WHOLE
- PASSION FRUIT, HALVED
- PURPLE BABY CARROTS, SCRUBBED AND HALVED LENGTHWAYS
- BLUEBERRIES

YELLOW

- YELLOW PEPPER, SEEDED AND SLICED
- MANGO, PEELED AND SLICED OR CUT INTO CUBES
- GOOSEBERRIES, WHOLE
- BABY POTATOES, SCRUBBED, HALVED AND ROASTED

GREEN

- BROCCOLI, BLANCHED
- CUCUMBER, SLICED INTO ROUNDS
- ROCKET, DRIZZLED IN OLIVE OIL
- OLIVES, IN A BOWL OF OLIVE OIL

ORANGE

- BUTTERNUT, SLICED INTO DISCS, SKIN ON AND ROASTED UNTIL GOLDEN AND DELICIOUS
- CARROTS, SCRUBBED AND CUT INTO BITE-SIZE STICKS
- ORANGES, SLICED OR SEGMENTED

SOURDOUGH PANCAKES

WITH SAUTÉED MUSHROOMS AND CARAMELISED ONION

SERVES: **2** | PREPARATION TIME: **10** MINUTES *(EXCLUDING RESTING TIME)* | COOKING TIME: **15** MINUTES

This recipe was a happy discovery in my kitchen. Making your own sourdough is so rewarding and making additional by-products such as these pancakes is the ultimate win. They are comforting and if you leave out the spring onion then you could even go the sweet route with some coconut sugar and cinnamon. Either way, give them a go because they are delicious!

SOURDOUGH PANCAKE BATTER

- 1½ CUPS SOURDOUGH STARTER (SEE PAGE 42)
- ½ CUP WATER
- 1 EGG
- 1 TABLESPOON OLIVE OIL, PLUS EXTRA
- ¼ CUP STONEGROUND BREAD FLOUR
- ½ CUP FINELY SLICED SPRING ONIONS
- 1 TEASPOON SALT

SAVOURY FILLING

- 1 RED ONION, FINELY SLICED INTO ROUNDS
- ¼ CUP BALSAMIC
- 2 TEASPOONS OLIVE OIL
- 2 LARGE BROWN MUSHROOMS AND/OR SHIMEJI MUSHROOMS, SLICED
- SALT AND PEPPER
- 1 HANDFUL ROCKET
- 100 GRAMS RICOTTA CHEESE

In a large mixing bowl, combine the sourdough starter with the water. Add the egg and olive oil and whisk until well combined. Add the flour and stir well, making sure all the lumps are whisked out. The batter should feel quite wet and soft. Let it rest for 30 minutes.

Add the spring onions and salt to the batter and stir. Add a little olive oil to a medium-sized non-stick frying pan over medium heat. Once hot, pour ½ cup of the batter into the hot pan. Swirl the pan to spread the batter so that it covers the surface. This gives the pancake a thin, crusty texture. Cook the pancake until golden brown – roughly 1 minute on each side. Once the pancake is ready, remove from the pan and stack on a plate. Repeat with the rest of the batter.

To make the filling, place the onion, balsamic and ¼ cup water into a medium-sized saucepan over medium heat. Bring to a simmer and let it reduce for roughly 15 minutes until the onion is soft and sticky. Once ready, set aside.

In the same frying pan you made the pancakes in, add the 2 teaspoons olive oil and the mushrooms. Season with salt and pepper and sauté for about 5 minutes until golden brown and the mushrooms are cooked through. Once ready, set aside.

Now it is time to assemble your pancakes. I start with adding the rocket, then the mushrooms and onions. I top it off with the ricotta (and a few extra slices of spring onion, if I'm in the mood) and then roll up. Enjoy!

FOR THE LITTLE ONES

I often speak about an 80/20 approach to eating – 80 per cent of the time focusing on eating healthy, real whole foods and 20 per cent allowing life to happen and enjoying that cupcake at your child's birthday party. This means eating plenty of vegetables and cutting out refined sugars and processed foods. Doing this for ourselves can be a lot easier than doing it for our children.

Parents are often stressed, busy and tired, and our unhealthy habits frequently get handed down to our children. Either that or we give into the battle of wills in the home when our children don't like the taste or texture of the vegetables they are given. I have seen first-hand how parents get tired after a few back and forths of 'eat your vegetables' – the children end up eating something unhealthy and the parents are just relieved they are eating anything at all. Truth be told, your children do not know what is best for them when it comes to their nutrition, and although it can seem impossibly hard at times, it is up to you to make sure they are eating food that really benefits their health.

Giving your child nutrient-dense food means stable blood sugar and, in turn, fewer mood swings, regular bowel movements and less brain fog. This ultimately results in a happier, healthier child who is able to concentrate better in school and has quality energy to move throughout their day. It's time for parents to take a stance and feed their little humans, the future of this planet, quality food. If we do so we are not only ensuring a better future for the planet, but we are also creating a generation of healthy children who will not be medication dependent and plagued with health issues such as diabetes. Giving your child a sugary soda and processed foods is, quite simply, unhealthy and harmful. If you have a picky eater, don't give in, get creative. Find real whole foods your child loves and prepare them in delicious ways. Less frozen, more fresh. Less processed, more real food.

- What attitude do you have towards healthy food and balanced living and do you share your thoughts openly with your children?

- How can you be more proactive in cooking your children healthier whole-food meals?

- What nutritional example is your child getting from school and how can you better support a healthier outcome?

HEALTH TIPS

- Not only should we question the chemicals in our environment and food for our own sake, but also for our children's. Do the baby products you use have a lot of chemicals? Natural baby products are where it's at and, although they can be more pricey, there are plenty that aren't. And, in the long run, what you save on your reusable diapers will make up for the initial spend on them. Not only is it better for babies, but for our planet too.
- Look after yourself the way you do your baby. Speak to yourself with care, feed yourself healthy real food and make sure you get plenty of sleep and water.

CHOCOLATE SPREAD

TWO WAYS TO SWEETNESS

SERVES: 6 | PREPARATION TIME: 10 MINUTES | COOKING TIME: 15 MINUTES

Sweetness is the key to finding a way to get your children to eat vegetables. And just like our mature palates, theirs can evolve and adapt to what you feed them. The exciting thing is that the sweetness doesn't have to come from refined sugars and processed foods. Getting creative with natural sugars means that you can get high-fibre vegetables into your child's diet. This recipe is an example of how, instead of removing a fun and tasty chocolate spread from their diet, you can replace it with something healthier that is just as tasty.

OPTION 1

3 CUPS RAW HAZELNUTS

½ CUP RAW CACAO POWDER

2–3 TABLESPOONS HONEY OR
MAPLE SYRUP

1 TEASPOON VANILLA PASTE

½ TEASPOON SALT

OPTION 2

400 GRAMS CHICKPEAS, COOKED (SEE
PAGE 24)

¼ CUP PURE PEANUT BUTTER OR NUT
BUTTER OF YOUR CHOICE

½ CUP RAW CACAO POWDER

1 TEASPOON VANILLA PASTE

3 TABLESPOONS HONEY OR MAPLE SYRUP

½ TEASPOON SALT

OPTION 1

Preheat the oven to 180 °C.

Place the hazelnuts onto a baking tray and pop them in the oven for 15 minutes, keeping an eye on them so that they don't burn. Once the nuts are heated, they will not only release their natural oils, but the oil will also loosen their skins. Transfer the nuts to a kitchen towel and rub vigorously. This will remove most of the skins. You can also rub them between your hands. Discard the skins and add the nuts to a food processor or blender.

Blend at a high speed for 10 minutes, scraping down the sides now and then, until a nut butter starts to form. If needed, add a tablespoon of warm water to help it along.

When you have achieved a buttery consistency with the blended nuts, add the cocoa, honey or maple syrup, vanilla paste and salt. If you find that your child is wanting a little more sweetness, then add a little more honey. Rather healthy sugars which the body can process than refined sugars combined with chemical nasties.

Blend on high speed for an additional 2 minutes. Store in an airtight container in the fridge for up to a week.

OPTION 2

Place all the ingredients into a high-speed blender and blend until smooth. If necessary, add a little water to loosen the consistency.

Spread on some brown toast or sourdough and see how your kids enjoy it! Store in an airtight container for up to 5 days in the fridge.

MINDFUL MUNCHIES

HEALTHY LUNCHBOX

SERVES: 1 | PREPARATION TIME: 20 MINUTES

I hope that this chapter will inspire you to make healthy, amazing food for your little ones. Going to school without proper nutrition can affect a child's ability to concentrate and focus in class. If your children are eating sugary cereal that has empty calories then they are not receiving the correct brain food. So often convenience trumps health and this can mean that nutrition falls by the wayside. Below are some easy and fun ideas to fill your children's lunchboxes, along with a delicious bean dip!

BEAN DIP

- 1 CUP BLACK BEANS, COOKED (SEE PAGE 24)
- ¼ RED ONION, SLICED
- ½ TEASPOON GROUND CUMIN
- JUICE OF 1 LIME
- 1 SMALL HANDFUL FRESH CORIANDER LEAVES
- SALT AND PEPPER

ITEMS FOR DIPPING

- ROSA TOMATOES
- SLICED CUCUMBER WITH A LITTLE SALT AND PEPPER
- BLANCHED BROCCOLI WITH A BIT OF OLIVE OIL AND SALT AND PEPPER
- BOILED EGG

OTHER LUNCHBOX IDEAS

- RICE CRACKERS AND HEALING HUMMUS (SEE PAGE 162)
- AVOCADO AND FETA SANDWICH
- DICED KIWI FRUIT
- ORANGE SEGMENTS
- BLUEBERRIES
- STRAWBERRIES
- SLICED APPLE WITH NUT BUTTER
- DAIRY-FREE DARK CHOCOLATE OR CHOCOLATE SPREAD (SEE PAGE 169)

BEAN DIP

Place all the ingredients into a blender and blend until you reach a chunky or smooth consistency, depending how your children like it. Serve with a selection of the suggested items for dipping.

For the rest of the lunchbox, come up with fun and colourful combinations of the suggested ingredients listed under other lunchbox ideas.

SNEAKY MUFFINS

SWEET POTATO AND SPINACH

MAKES: **12** STANDARD MUFFINS | PREPARATION TIME: **10** MINUTES | BAKING TIME: **25** MINUTES

This recipe is here to shine a light on meal prep for your little ones. The reality is that you don't always have time. When the going gets tough, a parent gets tougher. Dig deep and make the time to prep items that give you several meals from one cooking session.
These muffins not only sneak in the vegetables, but also have a natural sweetness from the sweet potato. Your children can grab one from the fridge or you can pop one into their lunchboxes. They keep for up to four days in the fridge and you can freeze them as well, making these muffins serious ammunition in a parent's artillery.

100 GRAMS SWEET POTATO, PEELED
    AND GRATED
1 CUP OAT FLOUR
1¼ CUPS BUCKWHEAT FLOUR, SIFTED
2 TEASPOONS BAKING POWDER
1 TEASPOON GROUND GINGER
½ TEASPOON SEA SALT
3 EGGS
2 HANDFULS BABY SPINACH
5 MEDJOOL DATES, PITTED
⅔ CUP PLAIN YOGHURT
½ CUP OLIVE OIL
2 TEASPOONS LEMON ZEST

TOPPING

3 TABLESPOONS MAPLE SYRUP OR HONEY
1 TABLESPOON OLIVE OIL
½ CUP PUMPKIN SEEDS

Preheat the oven to 200 °C. Line a muffin tray with 12 muffin cases.

In a large bowl, mix together the sweet potato, flours, baking powder, ginger and salt. Once combined, make a well in the centre of the mixture.

Place the eggs, spinach, dates, yoghurt, oil and lemon zest into a food processor and blend until well combined. Slowly pour this mixture into the centre of the potato mixture and gently fold it through until it is all incorporated. Do not overmix as it can make the muffins tough. Once combined, spoon the mixture into the muffin cases, filling them about three-quarters full.

Bake for 25 minutes or until the muffins spring back when touched. Once ready, remove from the oven and set aside to cool.

For the topping, combine the maple syrup or honey and the olive oil. Spoon a little on top of each cooled muffin and sprinkle on the pumpkin seeds so they stick.

TOP TIP

Get your kids into the kitchen and engage with them on how their food is made. Get them involved in making these muffins – they can sprinkle the pumpkin seeds on top or even spoon the batter into the muffin cases. Make it fun while making memories with them.

SWEET AND FLUFFY

BEETROOT AND SPINACH PANCAKES

SERVES: 4 | PREPARATION TIME: 15 MINUTES | COOKING TIME: 6 MINUTES EACH

Make eating a celebration, and make preparing your food fun! Linking your food to exciting stories, allowing your child to cook with you and crafting cool names for your food will inspire your child to connect with the process of making the food as well as eating it. Meals don't have to be boring and plain – make them come alive. Let your imagination inspire theirs and theme the food to their personalities!

PANCAKES

- 1 ROASTED BEETROOT (SEE PAGE 76) OR
  ½ CUP BABY SPINACH
- 2 EGGS
- 1 LARGE RIPE BANANA
- ¼ CUP ALMOND MILK OR MILK SUBSTITUTE
  OF YOUR CHOICE
- 30 GRAMS BUCKWHEAT FLOUR
- 25 GRAMS ROLLED OATS
- 20 GRAMS DESICCATED COCONUT
- ½ TEASPOON SALT
- ½ TEASPOON BAKING POWDER
- ½ TEASPOON GROUND CINNAMON
- 1 TEASPOON VANILLA PASTE
- 2 TABLESPOONS GHEE OR COCONUT OIL

TOPPINGS

- 2 TABLESPOONS MAPLE SYRUP
- 1 RIPE BANANA, SLICED
- 6 STRAWBERRIES, SLICED
- 1 HANDFUL BLUEBERRIES
- 1 TABLESPOON CHIA SEEDS

Choose either the roasted beetroot or baby spinach to give the pancakes the colour of your choice and blend it in a high-speed blender until smooth. If necessary, you can add a little water to help it along. Set aside.

Place the eggs, banana, milk, flour, oats, coconut, salt, baking powder, cinnamon and vanilla paste into a blender and blend until smooth. Add the blended spinach or beetroot to the batter and blend again until combined.

Heat 1 teaspoon of the ghee or coconut oil in a medium-sized frying pan over medium heat. Once hot, add a generous spoonful of pancake batter to the pan and swirl the pan a little to create the pancake. Cook for 2–3 minutes or until golden underneath and then flip it over, cooking for another 2–3 minutes. (Don't worry if it's a flop [excuse the pun]; the first one is always practice.) Remove from the pan and keep warm. Repeat with the rest of the batter.

Stack the pancakes and serve with the toppings of your choice.

TOP TIP

Divide the batter in half and mix the beetroot into one half and the spinach into the other.

CHOCOLATE BITES

CHOC CHIP COOKIES

MAKES: 15 | PREPARATION TIME: 15–20 MINUTES (*EXCLUDING 4 HOURS RESTING TIME*) | BAKING TIME: 10 MINUTES

Setting up healthy food habits from a young age and sharing your knowledge about food and nutrition will educate your child about the difference between good-quality and bad-quality food. Knowledge is power. Empower them to make healthier choices for themselves. These are ideally prepped the day before so they have sufficient rest time.

¾ CUP GHEE, COLD FROM FRIDGE

2 TABLESPOONS WATER

¼ CUP COCONUT SUGAR

¼ CUP UNREFINED BROWN SUGAR

1 LARGE EGG

1 TEASPOON VANILLA PASTE

1¼ CUPS GLUTEN-FREE FLOUR

¼ CUP RAW CACAO POWDER

1 CUP DAIRY-FREE DARK CHOCOLATE, ROUGHLY CHOPPED

Place the ghee, water and both sugars into the bowl of a stand mixer and beat at high speed for about 5 minutes until light and creamy.

Add the egg and vanilla paste, scrape down the sides and beat again for about 5 minutes until well combined.

Add the gluten-free flour and the cacao powder, 2 tablespoons at a time, mixing in between until well combined. The mixture should thicken to a soft dough-like consistency.

Fold through the chocolate pieces and then cover the dough and pop it into the fridge for a minimum of 4 hours or preferably overnight. Once chilled, you should be able to roll the dough into balls.

Preheat the oven to 180 °C. Line a baking tray with baking paper.

Using a tablespoon, scoop out even amounts of dough and roll them into balls just larger than a ping-pong ball. Place them on the baking tray, press lightly with a fork and allow 3 cm of space around them for when they bake and spread out.

Bake for 8–10 minutes or until the edges start to become golden brown. Once ready, allow to cool for 5 minutes on the tray before transferring to a cooling rack. Leave as is or melt some dark chocolate, drizzle it over the cookies and allow to set. Once cooled completely you can store the cookies in an airtight container. You can also freeze the balls of dough in a freezer-safe container and make cookies on demand – just add 5 minutes to the baking time.

SPAG BOWL

LENTIL BOLOGNESE WITH LOADED VEGGIE SAUCE

SERVES: 4 | PREPARATION TIME: 10 MINUTES | COOKING TIME: 50 MINUTES

Trying out vegetarian dishes for your children can be difficult, but it is worth it when you find a breakthrough point and something they enjoy. This dish is a new take on a classic that all kids love. You can swop out the wheat pasta for a variety of healthy alternatives from your local health store. Cook the sauce with love and give it time for the flavours to develop. Your kids will also enjoy any leftover lentil sauce for sloppy Joe's or on toast with some egg. The real challenge is making sure you don't finish it all in one go!

---

1 TABLESPOON COCONUT OIL

1 RED ONION, CHOPPED

2 CLOVES GARLIC, MINCED

110 GRAMS PORTOBELLO MUSHROOMS, CHOPPED

1 TABLESPOON TOMATO PASTE

1 MEDIUM-SIZED CARROT, SCRUBBED AND GRATED

1 SMALL STALK CELERY, CHOPPED

1 TEASPOON PAPRIKA

1 TEASPOON DRIED OREGANO

450 GRAMS CHERRY TOMATOES, HALVED

1 TABLESPOON COCONUT SUGAR

½ CUP UNCOOKED RED SPLIT LENTILS

½ CUP UNCOOKED BROWN LENTILS

2½ CUPS VEGETABLE STOCK

SALT AND PEPPER

125 GRAMS GLUTEN-FREE SPAGHETTI OR SPAGHETTI OF YOUR CHOICE

3 TABLESPOONS OLIVE OIL

2 TABLESPOONS NUTRITIONAL YEAST

½ CUP FRESH BASIL LEAVES OR PARSLEY

Heat the coconut oil in a medium-sized saucepan over medium heat. Add the onion and sauté for 5 minutes until translucent. Add the garlic and mushrooms and cook for an additional 5 minutes, stirring often. Add the tomato paste, carrot, celery, paprika and oregano. Cook down for 5 minutes, stirring often. Once the celery and carrot soften, add the tomatoes and sugar and mix well. Add the lentils and vegetable stock and bring the mixture to a simmer with the lid on. Cook for 35 minutes or until the lentils are al dente, verging on soft. Make sure to give the sauce a stir every 10 minutes. Once ready, season to taste.

While the sauce is cooking, prepare the spaghetti as per the packet instructions in salted water. Once ready, drain and set aside. Drizzle the olive oil over the spaghetti so that it doesn't stick together.

Serve the spaghetti topped with the lentil Bolognese sauce, sprinkled with the nutritional yeast and garnished with fresh basil or parsley.

PEACH'S PICKINGS

I'M MOVING TO SOLIDS — FOR THE LITTLEST LITTLE ONES

So often I speak to mothers who are stressed and confused about how and what their baby should be eating. The truth is, bottled baby food has hidden sugars and preservatives that you don't want to be feeding your baby if you can help it. The exciting thing is that when you cook for yourself you can actually cook for the baby and when you prepare for the baby you can prepare for yourself. For example, roast some butternut for yourself for a roasted butternut salad and then blend some of it for your baby with a little cinnamon and nut butter. Yum!

MORNING: CARROT CAKE OATS

SERVES: 1 | PREPARATION TIME: 10 MINUTES | COOKING TIME: 5 MINUTES

---

3 TABLESPOONS ROLLED
    OATS, BLENDED
½ CUP WATER
½ TEASPOON GROUND
    CINNAMON
1 SMALL CARROT, SCRUBBED
    AND GRATED
1 BANANA, PEELED AND MASHED
1 TEASPOON ALMOND BUTTER
1 TEASPOON CHIA SEEDS

If you want to cook the oats, place the oats and water into a small saucepan over medium heat. Bring to a slow simmer for 5 minutes. You also have the option to mix them together without cooking.

When the oats and water are mixed together, add the remaining ingredients and stir until well combined. Sprinkle with extra chia seeds, if desired, and serve warm or at room temperature.

NOON: GREENS AND GRAINS

SERVES: 1 | PREPARATION TIME: 5 MINUTES | COOKING TIME: 5–10 MINUTES

---

1 CUP UNCOOKED BROWN RICE
2 COURGETTES, TOPS REMOVED
¼ HEAD BROCCOLI
¼ HEAD CAULIFLOWER
¼ CUP FRESH OR FROZEN PEAS
1 HANDFUL BABY SPINACH
¼ CUP FRESH BASIL LEAVES

Cook the rice as per the packet instructions, without using salt.

While the rice is cooking, place the courgettes, broccoli and cauliflower into a steamer. Steam for 5–10 minutes until very soft when pierced with a fork.

Transfer the steamed vegetables, peas, spinach and basil to a food processor and pulse until you reach the desired consistency. Serve mixed together with the brown rice.

NIGHT: ROASTED REDS AND PASTA

SERVES: 1 | PREPARATION TIME: 10 MINUTES | COOKING TIME: 30 MINUTES

---

2 RED PEPPERS, SEEDED AND
    CHOPPED
1 CLOVE GARLIC
1 SMALL RED ONION, CHOPPED
200 GRAMS CHERRY TOMATOES
2 TEASPOONS MELTED
    COCONUT OIL
1 CUP CHICKPEA PASTA, COOKED

Preheat the oven to 180 °C.

Place the peppers, garlic, onion and tomatoes into a roasting tray. Add the coconut oil and toss until everything is coated. Roast for 30 minutes until soft and golden.

Meanwhile, cook the pasta as per the packet instructions, without salt.

Remove the vegetables from the oven and blend until smooth. Serve the pasta mixed with the sauce.

DESSERT

I want you to say to yourself: 'I give myself permission to indulge.'

Why? Because when you don't, you keep yourself in a feedback loop of guilt and shame when it comes to your eating habits. When you give yourself permission to indulge, you move away from the black-and-white thinking that can cause a lot of pain and anxiety when it comes to food. When you give yourself permission, the attachment that you have to indulgence can dissipate.

Every recipe in this chapter has been developed with the intention of indulging with love. That means all the ingredients are healthy and are good for your body.

If you change your thinking around food and your body, a whole new world can open up. You can eat in moderation and you can eat to nourish, not to harm. My wish for you is that food becomes a celebration and that, more than that, you heal your relationship with food and with yourself.

- What will happen if you don't take the steps towards a healthier life?

- What are you most proud of on your journey so far?

- What will your life look like after you have found balance and a healthier way of living?

HEALTH TIPS

- Green tea can help digestion and boost your metabolism. Having it in the morning or after a big meal is a wonderful way to do so.
- Make sure that the chocolate you buy is not only ethically sourced but is also free of chemicals. Most dairy milk chocolates are filled with nasties. I always go for dairy-free dark chocolate, which leaves me satisfied after a few blocks.
- Set yourself up for success when it comes to sugar cravings. Buy dates and keep them in the fridge, then when the sugar craving hits, grab two dates and a cup of tea. Yum!
- Take sleep seriously. The hours before midnight are the most important and spending your time on your phone in bed can affect your circadian rhythms. Put down the phone and rather read a book. In all seriousness, your emails, Instagram and Facebook can wait until the morning.

DOUBLE-DOWN CHOCOLATE

CHOC MACA MILKSHAKE OR ICE LOLLIES

SERVES: 2 OR MAKES 6 LOLLIES | PREPARATION TIME: 5 MINUTES
(EXCLUDING FREEZING TIME FOR LOLLIES)

It's simple. If they don't love the food, find a way to get them to love it. It just takes a bit of creativity, so get creative and make healthy spins on old classics. This is my take on a chocolate milkshake that is powered with superfoods and high in good fats. These will help your children concentrate better and give them quality energy. You can adjust the sweetness and play around with how you serve it as this recipe also freezes beautifully into ice lollies!

3 TABLESPOONS RAW CACAO POWDER
2 BANANAS, PEELED AND FROZEN
3 TABLESPOONS DESICCATED COCONUT
4 MEDJOOL DATES, PITTED
2 TABLESPOONS ALMOND BUTTER
1½ CUPS ALMOND OR COCONUT MILK
1 TEASPOON MACA POWDER

Place all the ingredients into a high-speed blender and blend until smooth. Add more liquid as required. Serve cold if you are having a milkshake or pour the liquid into ice-lolly moulds and freeze overnight for a refreshing and decadent treat!

VARIATION

Melt some dark chocolate and drizzle it over the top of the milkshake or unmoulded lollies to add an extra touch of decadence. Sprinkle with finely chopped nuts of choice.

TURNDOWN DROPS

LAVENDER AND HONEY WHITE CHOCOLATES

SERVES: 6 | PREPARATION TIME: 15 MINUTES |
COOKING TIME: 10 MINUTES (*EXCLUDING SETTING TIME IN FRIDGE*)

How often do you meditate, if at all? Meditation is a wonderful way to regulate the body's systems and to reconnect to self, spiritually, physically and emotionally. Meditation can improve blood pressure, heart rate and brain waves. It creates space where once there was noise. Try it in the morning or at night before bedtime to help wind down your body and prepare it for sleep. The lavender in this recipe also has a calming effect on the body so having one of these chocolates with a chamomile tea just before bed will support a good night's sleep.

1 CUP CACAO BUTTER

¼ CUP COCONUT OIL

3 TEASPOONS DRIED LAVENDER

1 CUP CASHEW NUT BUTTER

¼ CUP HONEY

2 TABLESPOONS MESQUITE POWDER

1 TABLESPOON LACUMA POWDER

1 TEASPOON VANILLA PASTE

1 TEASPOON BEE POLLEN (OPTIONAL)

4 DRIED APRICOTS, FINELY SLICED
(OPTIONAL)

Melt the cacao butter over a double boiler. Once melted, fold in the coconut oil to ensure it melts and add 2 teaspoons of the lavender. Gently warming it will release its calming flavour. Once combined, remove from the heat and transfer the mixture to a food processor or blender. Blend on a medium speed for about 15 seconds. Add the cashew butter, honey, mesquite powder, lacuma powder and vanilla paste and blend until smooth.

Using a mini-muffin tray or silicone mould of your choice, add a small sprinkle of bee pollen (if using) followed by the apricots (if using) and the chocolate mixture. If you are using a muffin tin then only fill it halfway. Once you have filled the mould, sprinkle the remaining lavender on top. Pop the chocolates into the fridge and allow to set for a minimum of 4 hours.

These chocolates melt quickly so only take them out of the fridge just before you eat them.

BANOFFEE PIE

CARAMEL, BANANA AND COCONUT WHIP

SERVES: 6 | PREPARATION TIME: 15 MINUTES (*EXCLUDING CHILLING TIME*) | BAKING TIME: 15 MINUTES

Here is a fun fact. For every delicious meal you have had that is unhealthy, there is an equally tasty yet healthy equivalent. Yes, that means you can have your cake and eat it. All you have to do is put in the effort to make it a cake that is healthier, with less sugar and refined processed ingredients. I used to think that I would never be able to indulge if I wanted to be healthy. The fact is, it's the opposite. Indulgence is part of healthy, balanced living.

The different elements of this recipe need time to set in the fridge, so making it the day before is recommended. Take note that the whip will only work if you have chilled your coconut cream in the can. Do not shake the can before use and make sure it is well chilled. You are only going to use the solid part that separates from the liquid in the can and rises to the top.

---

3 BANANAS, SLICED
80 GRAMS DAIRY-FREE DARK CHOCOLATE, GRATED
1 TEASPOON GROUND CINNAMON

CRUST

5 MEDJOOL DATES, PITTED
1 CUP ROLLED OATS
½ CUP DESICCATED COCONUT
½ CUP RAW ALMONDS
½ TEASPOON SALT
¼ CUP MAPLE SYRUP
¼ CUP MELTED COCONUT OIL
2 TEASPOONS LEMON JUICE
ZEST OF ½ LEMON

CARAMEL

20 LARGE MEDJOOL DATES, PITTED
  AND SOAKED IN WARM WATER FOR
  15 MINUTES THEN DRAINED
PINCH OF SALT
3 TABLESPOONS SMOOTH
  ALMOND BUTTER
1 TEASPOON LEMON JUICE
1 TEASPOON GROUND CINNAMON
2 TEASPOONS VANILLA PASTE

WHIP

½ CUP COCONUT CREAM SOLID, CHILLED
  IN THE FRIDGE OVERNIGHT OR FOR AT
  LEAST 4 HOURS
1 TABLESPOON MAPLE SYRUP (OR XYLITOL
  IF YOU WANT THE CREAM TO STAY WHITE)
¼ TEASPOON AGAR AGAR POWDER

Preheat the oven to 180 °C.

For the crust, place the dates in a high-speed food processor or blender and blend until smooth. Add the oats, coconut and almonds and blend until it forms a fine crumb. Add the remaining ingredients and blend until well combined.

Gently press the crust into a 20 cm pie pan or individual tart bases, preferably with a removable base. Pop the pie pan into the oven and bake for 10–15 minutes until golden brown. Once ready, remove from the oven and allow to cool completely.

For the caramel, place all the ingredients into a high-speed food processor or blender and blend until smooth. If the mixture gets stuck, add 1 tablespoon hot water. Once smooth, refrigerate for at least 10 minutes.

For the whip, place the solid coconut cream into a stand mixer with the whisk attachment and whisk on high speed. Once stiff peaks start to form, add the remaining ingredients and whisk until well combined. Cover the bowl and pop it into the fridge for 20 minutes.

Once all the elements are chilled you can assemble the pie. Start by spooning the caramel onto the crust base. Spread it to create an even layer, and then top it with the banana slices (dust with cinnamon or grated chocolate, if you like). Top with lashings of the whip and sprinkle over the grated chocolate and a dusting of cinnamon.

Pop it back into the fridge to set for a minimum of 2 hours, then serve.

CHOCOLATE BARS

CRUNCHY CARAMEL AND CRISP COCONUT

SERVES: 6 | PREPARATION TIME: 1 HOUR *(EXCLUDING SETTING TIME)* | BAKING TIME: 12 MINUTES

Looking after your relationships is vital to good health. Let go of grudges and cut out toxic friendships. Allow your heart to heal and bring good energy into your life. When you do, share these chocolate caramel coconut bars around the table. This recipe is inspired by my social circle and their passion for healthy indulgences. We could never live without a glass of wine and chocolate!

1 CUP DESICCATED COCONUT

½ CUP ALMOND FLOUR

¼ CUP COCONUT OIL

2 TABLESPOONS HONEY OR MAPLE SYRUP

2 TEASPOONS VANILLA PASTE

1 TEASPOON MALDON SALT, PLUS A LITTLE
  EXTRA FOR TOPPING

¾ CUP MAPLE SYRUP

½ CUP COCONUT CREAM SOLID (SEE
  PAGE 189)

2 TABLESPOONS CASHEW NUT BUTTER OR
  ALMOND BUTTER

300 GRAMS DAIRY-FREE DARK CHOCOLATE

1 TABLESPOON COCONUT OIL

Preheat the oven to 180 °C. Line a 20 x 30 cm baking tin with baking paper.

To make the biscuit layer, place the desiccated coconut, almond flour, ¼ cup coconut oil, honey or maple syrup, 1 teaspoon of the vanilla paste and the Maldon salt into a stand mixer and mix until well combined. Once combined, press the mixture onto the base of the baking tin to form an even layer. Pop it into the oven and bake for 10–12 minutes until slightly golden. Remove from the oven and let it cool.

Meanwhile, place the ¾ cup maple syrup and the solid coconut cream into a medium-sized saucepan over medium to high heat. Bring the mixture to a boil and boil for 15 minutes, stirring often. The mixture should start to thicken and darken, forming the caramel sauce. Once this happens, remove it from the heat and stir in the cashew or almond butter and the remaining teaspoon of vanilla paste. Cool slightly before spooning it on top of the biscuit layer in the baking tin. Spread the layer evenly and then pop it into the freezer for 30 minutes or until completely set.

Melt the chocolate over a double boiler. Once melted, fold through the 1 tablespoon coconut oil. Remove from the heat and allow it to cool for 10 minutes.

Remove the baking tin from the freezer. Cut into bars about 2–3 cm wide. Using two forks to hold the bars, dunk them into the melted chocolate, making sure they are completely covered.

Place the chocolate bars on a lined baking tray. Before the chocolate cools, sprinkle a little extra Maldon salt on top (you can even add decorative drizzle of melted chocolate, if you like). Pop them back into the freezer for an additional 30 minutes to set.

You can keep them in the fridge for about 4 days, but they're hard to resist!

PRINCESS BITES

PEANUT BUTTER AND OAT CHOCOLATE-DIPPED COOKIES

MAKES: 35 COOKIES | PREPARATION TIME: 25 MINUTES | BAKING TIME: 15 MINUTES

Peanut butter is a power house of healthy fats and protein. Peanuts can help keep your blood sugar stable and are high in B vitamins. When buying peanut butter, look out for one without added sugar, preservatives or palm oil.

1¼ CUPS PEANUT BUTTER

1 CUP PACKED MEDJOOL DATES, PITTED

2 TEASPOONS VANILLA PASTE

½ CUP ROLLED OATS

2 EGGS

½ TEASPOON GROUND CARDAMOM

ZEST OF ½ ORANGE (OPTIONAL)

250 GRAMS DAIRY-FREE DARK CHOCOLATE

80 GRAMS RAW OR SALTED PEANUTS,
    ROASTED (SEE PAGE 24) AND
    FINELY CHOPPED

Preheat the oven to 180 °C. Line a baking tray with baking paper and set aside.

Place the peanut butter, dates and vanilla paste into a food processor and blend until smooth. If you do not have a powerful processor then I recommend doing this in batches and combining it all at the end. Add the oats, eggs, cardamom and orange zest (if using) and blend until combined.

Scoop out ½ tablespoons of the cookie dough and roll even-sized balls, slightly smaller than a ping-pong ball. Place them on the baking tray, spaced well apart to allow room for spreading, and press them flat with the back of a fork.

Pop the cookies into the oven and bake for 10–15 minutes until golden brown. You don't want to over bake them so make sure you keep an eye on them. Once ready, remove from the oven and allow to cool on the tray for 5 minutes before transferring them to a cooling rack to cool completely.

While the cookies are cooling, melt the chocolate over a double boiler and pop the peanuts into a small bowl. Once the chocolate has melted, dunk the edges of the cookies in the chocolate first and then into the peanuts. Place them on the cooling rack to set and then tuck in!

VARIATION

Press edible flowers onto the cookies just before baking to add that extra-special touch.

HONEY CRUNCH

BAKED BAKLAVA

SERVES: 6 | PREPARATION TIME: 20 MINUTES | BAKING TIME: 1 HOUR

This is a great dessert to make the day before and let stand in the fridge for the flavours to develop. The syrup can be made with coconut sugar or unrefined brown sugar. I use coconut sugar because I like the caramel richness that it offers. The large variety of nuts means that this dish will encourage you to chew, which in turn aids digestion. The nuts are also high in fibre and vitamins.

150 GRAMS SHELLED RAW PISTACHIO NUTS
100 GRAMS RAW ALMONDS
100 GRAMS RAW WALNUTS
1 TEASPOON GROUND CARDAMOM
¼ TEASPOON GRATED FRESH NUTMEG
1 TEASPOON GROUND CINNAMON
1 PACKET PHYLLO PASTRY
½ CUP OLIVE OIL OR GHEE FOR BRUSHING
   THE PASTRY

SYRUP

¾ CUP COCONUT SUGAR
¾ CUP WATER
ZEST AND STRAINED JUICE OF 1 ORANGE
2 TABLESPOONS ROSE WATER
¼ CUP HONEY
1 TEASPOON VANILLA PASTE

TOP TIPS FOR WORKING
WITH PHYLLO PASTRY

- Don't let the pastry dry out, cover it with a damp cloth while working.

- Work quickly.

- Don't worry if it tears.

- Make sure every layer gets a light coating of olive oil or ghee.

Place all the nuts into a large frying pan over medium heat. Toast for roughly 5 minutes until golden brown. Keep an eye on the nuts and stir often as they can burn easily. Once toasted, pop the nuts onto a chopping board and roughly chop so that the nuts are just bigger than lentils. You don't want to chop them too finely. Set aside in a medium-sized bowl.

Add the cardamom, nutmeg and cinnamon to the same frying pan and lightly toast the spices for 2–3 minutes until aromatic. Add the spices to the nuts and mix well.

Preheat the oven to 180 °C.

For the next part, you will need to move quickly as phyllo pastry can dry out. Roll open your phyllo pastry after it has defrosted. Take one sheet of phyllo pastry and place it on your cleaned work surface. Brush it generously with olive oil or ghee. Repeat this with the remaining sheets until they are all layered one on top of the other and oiled in between. Spoon the nut mixture along the bottom of the top sheet of phyllo forming a long sausage across the length of the pastry. Starting at the bottom, tightly roll the phyllo pastry over the nut mixture. As you roll, brush the unoiled parts of the pastry with olive oil or ghee. You should end up with a long sausage stuffed with nuts. Shape the sausage into a spiral with your hands. Be careful not to break the pastry, but if you do, it should be covered by the spiral shape. Place the spiral in a deep round baking dish, preferable a cosy fitted one so that the spiral holds together.

Pop the dish into the oven and bake for 45–50 minutes until all the layers are golden brown and crunchy.

While the baklava is baking, place the coconut sugar and water into a saucepan and simmer for 15 minutes. Add the orange zest, strained orange juice, rose water, honey and vanilla paste and stir. Simmer for an additional 5–10 minutes until syrupy, then remove from the heat.

Once the baklava has baked, remove it from the oven. Add the syrup immediately by spooning it evenly all over. This step must be done while the baklava is still hot.

Leave the baklava to cool, uncovered or it will go soggy, and then store it in the fridge or serve it hot and ready! Garnish with extra finely chopped nuts of choice, sesame seeds and/or edible flowers, if desired.

TEA TIME

SWEET POTATO BUNDT CAKELETTES

SERVES: 10 | PREPARATION TIME: 35 MINUTES | BAKING TIME: 25 MINUTES

This recipe is a delight to make for a tea party. Each little bundt cake is a treat and a perfect portion size. If you don't have a mini bundt cake pan then you can use a doughnut or cupcake pan, or a 15 cm cake pan. Just keep an eye on the baking time as it may vary by up to 10 minutes. You want the sponge to be light, fluffy and indulgent!

1 KILOGRAM WHITE SWEET POTATO,
PEELED AND CUT INTO 3 CM CUBES

½ CUP GHEE OR COCONUT OIL

100 GRAMS COCONUT SUGAR

1 VANILLA POD, SEEDS SCRAPED OUT OR
1 TABLESPOON VANILLA PASTE

1 TEASPOON GROUND CARDAMOM

2 TABLESPOONS DARK RUM (OPTIONAL)

2 EGGS OR VEGAN EGG REPLACEMENT

70 GRAMS SPELT OR GLUTEN-FREE FLOUR

1 TEASPOON BAKING POWDER

¼ CUP WATER

CARAMEL SAUCE

1 TABLESPOON ARROWROOT OR
CORNSTARCH

2 MEDJOOL DATES, PITTED AND
FINELY CHOPPED

1¼ CUPS COCONUT CREAM SOLID (SEE
PAGE 189)

¾ CUP COCONUT SUGAR

1 TEASPOON VANILLA PASTE OR HALF
THE SEEDS OF THE VANILLA POD
FROM ABOVE

¼ TEASPOON SALT

Pop the sweet potato cubes into a steamer and steam for 15–20 minutes or until soft when pierced with a fork. If you do not have a steamer you can boil the sweet potato and drain once soft.

Transfer the sweet potato to a large bowl and mash it. Whisk in the ghee or coconut oil, coconut sugar, vanilla, cardamom and rum (if using) until well combined. Break in the eggs, one at a time, and mix well after each addition. Alternatively, add the egg replacement. Mix in the flour and baking powder until just combined. If the mixture is too thick and pasty, add the ¼ cup of water. You want a batter-like consistency.

Preheat the oven to 180 °C. Grease your mini bundt cake pan.

Pour the batter into the prepared cake pan. Bake the bundt cakes in the oven for 20–25 minutes or until a toothpick comes out clean when the bundt cakes are pierced. Once ready, remove the cakes from the pan and allow to cool on a cooling rack.

While the cakes are baking, make the caramel sauce. Place the arrowroot or cornstarch, dates and solid coconut cream into a high-speed blender and blend until smooth.

Place the coconut sugar and the coconut cream mixture into a small saucepan over medium heat. Bring to a simmer and whisk continuously for 5–7 minutes until it starts to thicken and darken in colour. Don't let the mixture boil. The caramel is ready when it becomes dark and glossy. Once ready, remove it from the heat and fold through the vanilla and salt. Taste and adjust as needed – adding more vanilla, salt or coconut cream if you want a lighter colour. Allow to cool. If the sauce isn't smooth and creamy, feel free to put it through another round of blending.

Once the bundt cakes have cooled, dunk them in the caramel sauce and allow to set. These cakes keep very well in the fridge for up to a week!

CRUMBLE CAKE

CHERRY AND ORANGE

SERVES: 6 | PREPARATION TIME: 20 MINUTES | BAKING TIME: 1 HOUR

Everyone wants to be able to have their cake and eat it. With this recipe, you have found just that. It has the ultimate satisfaction that comes with a moist, rich cake and all the benefits of sweetness that come when baking fruits, especially cherries. I hope that you will give it a go and substitute your refined sugary standard cakes with a cake of this nature. After all, celebrating without guilt is utter magic!

FILLING

500 GRAMS FRESH CHERRIES, PITTED

1 TABLESPOON ORANGE ZEST

25 GRAMS COCONUT SUGAR

CRUMBLE

35 GRAMS WHOLEMEAL SPELT FLOUR

25 GRAMS COCONUT SUGAR

½ TEASPOON SALT

40 GRAMS GHEE OR BUTTER, COLD AND DICED INTO CUBES

50 GRAMS RAW WALNUTS, TOASTED AND ROUGHLY CHOPPED

DOUGH

125 GRAMS GHEE OR BUTTER

110 GRAMS DEMERARA SUGAR OR UNREFINED BROWN SUGAR

2 EGGS OR VEGAN EGG REPLACEMENT

1 TEASPOON VANILLA PASTE

1 TEASPOON CRACKED BLACK PEPPER

85 GRAMS WHOLEMEAL SPELT FLOUR

85 GRAMS SPELT FLOUR

1½ TEASPOONS BAKING POWDER

¼ TEASPOON SALT

Preheat the oven to 180 °C. Grease a 15 cm cake tin with coconut oil or ghee.

For the filling, mix together the cherries, orange zest and coconut sugar in a bowl and set aside.

For the crumble, place all the ingredients, except the walnuts, into a food processor and pulse until a coarse crumb has formed. Add the nuts and pulse once or twice to combine. Transfer the crumble to a bowl and pop it into the fridge until you need it.

Now it's time to make the dough. Whisk together the ghee or butter and sugar until creamy. Add the eggs (or egg replacement), one at a time, and whisk until just combined. Add the vanilla paste, black pepper, flours, baking powder and salt and whisk until combined. Don't over work the dough.

Spoon the dough into the cake tin and even out the surface with a spatula. Spread the cherry filling evenly onto the dough. Sprinkle the crumble on top of the filling, making sure everything is evenly covered.

Pop the cake onto the middle rack of the oven and bake for 1 hour. It is ready when a skewer inserted in the centre comes out clean. If the crumble darkens too quickly, slightly reduce the heat in your oven and keep an eye on it.

Once ready, remove from the oven and allow to cool fully in the tin before gently removing the cake. Serve with extra fresh cherries, if desired.

UNDER ORCHARD

SPICED APPLE LOAF WITH HAZELNUTS

SERVES: 6 | PREPARATION TIME: 15 MINUTES | BAKING TIME: 45 MINUTES

Baked fruit can be a thing of beauty. It is such a wonderful way to add natural sugar into a recipe and often results in a gooey, sticky pudding. Playing around with a variety of fruits can be so much fun. You could even subtitute the apples with pears in this recipe.

1 SMALL APPLE, CORED AND THINLY
   SLICED INTO WEDGES
5 TABLESPOONS DARK MUSCOVADO
   SUGAR
½ CUP COCONUT SUGAR
¼ CUP COCONUT OIL
¼ CUP COCONUT MILK
1 TABLESPOON APPLE CIDER VINEGAR
1 CUP SPELT FLOUR
1 TEASPOON BAKING POWDER
¼ TEASPOON BICARBONATE OF SODA
½ TEASPOON SALT
½ TEASPOON GROUND GINGER
½ TEASPOON GROUND CINNAMON
½ TEASPOON GROUND CLOVES
¼ TEASPOON GRATED FRESH NUTMEG
¼ TEASPOON GROUND CARDAMOM
1 LARGE APPLE, CORED AND CHOPPED
   INTO SMALL CUBES
2 TABLESPOONS MAPLE SYRUP
80 GRAMS RAW HAZELNUTS, ROASTED (SEE
   PAGE 24) AND ROUGHLY CHOPPED
6 BABY TOFFEE APPLES (OPTIONAL)

SYRUP

2 TABLESPOONS COCONUT SUGAR
ZEST AND JUICE OF 1 ORANGE
1 TABLESPOON WATER

Preheat the oven to 180 °C. Grease and line a 25 x 13 cm loaf tin.

Once you have lined the tin, place the apple wedges in a fish-scale pattern on the bottom. Sprinkle 1 tablespoon of the dark muscovado sugar over the apples and set aside.

Using a stand mixer with the whisk attachment, whisk together the coconut sugar, coconut oil and coconut milk. Add the vinegar and mix.

In a separate bowl, combine the flour, baking powder, bicarbonate of soda, salt and all the spices. Add the wet ingredients to the dry ingredients and combine until the batter is smooth. Do not over whisk.

In another bowl, combine the apple cubes, maple syrup and hazelnuts. Add this mixture to the cake batter and fold through. Pour the batter into the prepared tin and pop it in the oven for 40–45 minutes or until a toothpick inserted into the centre comes out clean.

Meanwhile, combine the ingredients for the syrup in a small saucepan over medium heat and simmer for 5 minutes until the sugar has dissolved.

Once the cake is ready, remove from the oven and let it cool in the tin for 10 minutes. Pour the syrup over the cake and then leave it in the tin for another 20 minutes. Once cooled, turn the cake out of the tin so that the apple wedges are on the top.

Set a cooling rack over a roasting tray. Pop the baby apples onto the cooling rack ready for the caramel to be poured over them. Place the remaining 4 tablespoons muscovado sugar and 2 tablespoons water in a small saucepan over medium heat. When the sugar starts to bubble, swirl the pan and let the caramel develop. Don't let the sugar burn so keep an eye on it. Once it starts to reach a sticky consistency, pour the caramel over the baby apples and allow to set.

Decorate your cake with the baby toffee apples (if using) and enjoy!

CHEESECAKES

ZESTY LIME AND CASHEW NUT

SERVES: 12 | PREPARATION TIME: 10 MINUTES (*EXCLUDING SETTING TIME*) | BAKING TIME: 12 MINUTES

Making vegan cheesecake is testament to the fact that plant-based food can be absolutely mind-blowingly yummy. This recipe is such a win because you can replace the lime juice with a cup of fresh or frozen blueberries and make a berry cheesecake. I love the zesty zing that you get with this recipe, not to mention the high hit of vitamin C. You can make this recipe as individual cheesecakes or you can prepare it in a 15 cm tart tin. Just make sure that you do it the day before as it is best when it has had a decent amount of time to set in the fridge.

BASE

- ½ CUP RAW ALMONDS
- ½ CUP RAW CASHEW NUTS
- 8 MEDJOOL DATES, PITTED AND ROUGHLY CHOPPED
- 3 TABLESPOONS DESICCATED COCONUT
- ¼ CUP COCONUT OIL
- 2 TABLESPOONS BUCKWHEAT, TOASTED (SEE PAGE 24)

FILLING

- 1 TEASPOON AGAR AGAR POWDER OR VEGAN GELATINE
- 1 TABLESPOON JUST-BOILED WATER
- 1 CUP RAW CASHEW NUTS, SOAKED OVERNIGHT OR FOR AT LEAST 4 HOURS IN WARM WATER
- 1 CUP COCONUT MILK
- ¼ CUP COCONUT OIL
- ½ CUP FRESH LIME JUICE
- ½ CUP MAPLE SYRUP
- 1 TEASPOON VANILLA PASTE
- 1½ TABLESPOONS LIME ZEST

Preheat the oven to 180 °C. Grease a 15 cm tart tin or 12-hole muffin tin.

Place all the ingredients for the base into a high-speed food processor or blender and blend until you get a fine crumb. Spoon the base into the prepared tin and flatten it with your fingers. Pop the tin into the oven and bake for 12 minutes until golden brown. Once ready, remove from the oven and allow to cool.

For the filling, place the agar agar powder or vegan gelatine and hot water into a small dish and stir until dissolved. Place all the ingredients, including the dissolved agar agar but excluding ½ tablespoon of the lime zest (save this for decorating), into a high-speed blender and blend until smooth. Taste and adjust as needed. For more sweetness add maple syrup, for more sourness add lime.

Pour the filling over the cooled base. Once the tin has been filled, gently lift and tap it down on the counter to knock out any bubbles. Sprinkle with the remaining lime zest and pop it into the fridge to set for a minimum of 4 hours or preferably overnight.

COLD COLLECTIVE

A NEST OF NICE CREAMS

SERVES: 4 | PREPARATION TIME: 10 MINUTES | FREEZING TIME: 2–3 HOURS

Nice cream is my go-to indulgence. I always have frozen banana in the freezer and using that as a base means that you can really go wild with different flavours. From chcocolate and peanut butter to fresh fruity flavours there is a little something for everyone. They are also wonderful to share with children as they are sweet and high in potassium, so you are winning either way with nutrients and happy smiles.

DRAGON FRUIT

- 1 CUP PINK DRAGON FRUIT, CUBED
- 7 BANANAS, PEELED AND FROZEN
- 2 MEDJOOL DATES, PITTED AND ROUGHLY CHOPPED
- ¼ CUP COCONUT MILK
- 1 TABLESPOON MAPLE SYRUP
- 1 TABLESPOON CACAO NIBS OR DAIRY-FREE DARK CHOCOLATE CHIPS

PASSION FRUIT

- 7 BANANAS, PEELED AND FROZEN
- 1 SMALL HANDFUL FRESH MINT LEAVES
- ¼ CUP COCONUT MILK
- PULP FROM 8 PASSION FRUIT

MANGO AND BERRIES

- 1 CUP FROZEN MANGO
- 2 BANANAS, PEELED AND FROZEN (OPTIONAL – IF YOU WISH TO OMIT THE BANANA, ADD 1 MORE CUP OF MANGO)
- ½ CUP FROZEN RASPBERRIES
- ⅓ CUP FROZEN BLUEBERRIES
- SQUEEZE OF FRESH LIME
- ¼ CUP COCONUT MILK

TAHINI PINEAPPLE

- 6 TABLESPOONS TAHINI
- 7 BANANAS, PEELED AND FROZEN
- 1 TABLESPOON MAPLE SYRUP
- 1 TEASPOON VANILLA PASTE
- ½ CUP ALMOND MILK
- 2 MEDJOOL DATES, PITTED
- 60 GRAMS DRIED OR FRESH PINEAPPLE, CHOPPED INTO SMALL PIECES

DRAGON FRUIT

Place the dragon fruit, bananas, dates, coconut milk and maple syrup into a high-speed food processor and blend together. Once creamy, add the cocoa nibs or chocolate chips and pulse until evenly distributed in the nice cream. You don't want to chop these up too finely. Spoon the nice cream into a freezer-safe container and freeze for a minimum of 3 hours.

PASSION FRUIT

Place the bananas, mint and coconut milk into a high-speed food processor and blend until creamy. Fold through the passion fruit pulp and spoon the mixture into a freezer-safe container. Smooth the top of the nice cream and pop it into the freezer for 2 hours. Serve with a dollop of passion fruit pulp, if desired.

MANGO AND BERRIES

Place all the ingredients into a high-speed food processor and blend until smooth and creamy. Spoon the nice cream into a freezer-safe container and freeze for a minimum of 3 hours.

TAHINI PINEAPPLE

Place the tahini, bananas, maple syrup, vanilla paste and almond milk into a high-speed food processor and blend until smooth and creamy. Add the dates and pineapple and pulse until bits of fruit are mixed in. Don't blend them completely. Spoon the nice cream into a freezer-safe container and freeze for a minimum of 3 hours. Sprinkle over some chia seeds when serving, if desired.

RECIPE INDEX